DO YOU GET IT?

A Journey of a New Mom with Brain Cancer

Dear Ron & Danielle,
Thanks for all your support throughout my journeys. We appreciate your sense of humour & friendship.
- Pei

LIN-PEI DE SOUZA

DO YOU GET IT?
Copyright © 2017 by Lin-Pei De Souza

Printed in Canada

ISBN: 978-1-4866-1412-7

Word Alive Press
131 Cordite Road, Winnipeg, MB R3W 1S1
www.wordalivepress.ca

MIX
Paper from
responsible sources
FSC® C103567

Library and Archives Canada Cataloguing in Publication

De Souza, Lin-Pei, author
      Do you get it? : a journey of a new mom with brain cancer / Lin-Pei De Souza.

Issued in print and electronic formats.
ISBN 978-1-4866-1412-7 (paperback).--ISBN 978-1-4866-1413-4 (ebook)

      1. De Souza, Lin-Pei--Health. 2. Pregnancy--Psychological aspects. 3. Pregnant women--Religious life. 4. Brain--Cancer--Psychological aspects. 5. Cancer--Patients--Religious life.
6. Brain--Cancer--Patients--Ontario--London--Biography.
I. Title.

RC280.B7D4 2016   616.99'4810092   C2016-906486-7
                                                                          C2016-906487-5

DEDICATION

To my faithful husband, Ivan, who tirelessly helped me through an exhausting cancer journey and a rewarding parenting journey: your wisdom, faith, and love keep me alive and our marriage strong.

To my sweet daughter, Genevieve: you are my twinkling star, and I love you very much. This book is especially for you to remember how much you mean to Dada and me.

CONTENTS

Part 2 – Supplementary Information

Part 3 – How I Got It

ACKNOWLEDGEMENTS

I sincerely thank my husband, Ivan, for using his good memory to help me recall when I lost consciousness and when I forgot details at appointments and for editing this book to ensure accuracy. I am thankful for his patience when repeating himself over and over again so that I could "get it."

I also thank all my diligent editors who gave me constructive comments and suggestions for revisions. I am grateful for their input and contribution to this book.

I also want to thank all my moral, spiritual, and financial supporters, who've given me hope to survive and endure a difficult yet rewarding cancer and parenting journey.

Disclaimer

Medications cited in this book are prescribed by the author's medical team. Over-the-counter medications were personally chosen by the author. Mentions of medication in this book do not indicate that these same medications will work for other individuals. The author does not advocate for any drug manufacturer or distributor and only mentions drug names to be specific and clear. Individuals are strongly encouraged to obtain expert advice from their own medical team about appropriate medications.

Some names are not specifically mentioned, to protect the privacy and confidentiality of the individuals. Where specific names are mentioned, the author has obtained the individual's approval to do so.

All website references were valid and accurately identified at the time of writing this book.

INTRODUCTION

Have you ever dreamed about your future with grand plans and hopes? I dreamed a grand dream of being a famous architect with a good husband and several kids. That was *my* dream; unfortunately, it was not the will of God. When I surrendered to God's will and plan, I found that His plan was a lot better than what I had conceived.

God is simply brilliant.

My husband (Ivan) and I are immigrants to Canada. I am Chinese and was born in Kuala Lumpur, Malaysia. My husband is Goan and was born in Kenya, Africa. Both our countries of origin were British colonies, so we could speak and/or write in English before we came to Canada. Both our families settled in Rexdale, a northwest area of Greater Toronto. A few years later, my family moved to Mississauga, about 25 km away. We continued attending high school in Rexdale. When Ivan graduated from high school, his family also moved to Mississauga, because that was the growth area outside of Toronto.

I met Ivan in high school. We hung around with each other quite a bit, but I would never have imagined that he was "my type." As time passed, I realized he was kind, gentle, wise, loving, and considerate, and he loved kids—excellent qualities for a spouse. Suffice it to say, we began dating when we were both in different universities. I studied at the University of Toronto while Ivan was at McMaster University in Hamilton. A long-distance relationship helped us to solidify our connection.

After we had dated for seven years, Ivan proposed marriage, and a year later we married. Not long after, our family and friends started to ask us when we would start a family. I just replied, "It will happen when it happens." I recalled one of the readings from our wedding, "There is an appointed time for everything, and a time for every affair under the heavens. A time to give birth, and a time to die" (Ecclesiastes 3:1–2). They stopped asking after a few years, realizing that the question was very intrusive on our personal lives. We wondered ourselves too and knew that the situation was in God's hands.

We now live in London, Ontario. We like to be active and busy. Ivan travelled several days a week and stayed overnight away from London. I worked busily and kept very long office hours. We both enjoyed our jobs and loved to take vacations to get away from busy work life.

However, in time, we realized that we are never fully in control of our whole lives. People we meet, places we visit, and all of our life experiences affect our lives. We may not realize that, as much as we want to believe that we are indeed in control, we really are not the masters of our own destiny. The true master and controller is God. I always liked to feel in control of my life. I was humbled and physically brought down to my knees to see that God was always watching over me.

This book tells of my journey and how life changed after I got pregnant and found out I had a terminal illness. My hope is that it will help the reader to understand our journey as parents, a patient, and a caregiver.

So much happened to us in such a short time that it is very difficult to put all my feelings and thoughts on paper. I attempted to do so in this book, which has three parts. In part 1, Our Roller-Coaster Journey, I describe our experiences of becoming new parents and learning about my illness. Part 2, Supplementary Information, provides more details of critical aspects of my family's journey. Finally, in part 3, How I Got It, I summarize what I learned from all the ups and downs in life.

Our journey was like a true roller-coaster ride. I firmly believe that our faith carried us through the twists and turns. Share our journey with us as I explain how we coped with life's difficulties and survived.

PART 1
OUR ROLLER-COASTER JOURNEY

1. God's Big Plan

My future husband, Ivan, and I became good friends in high school. My sister is one year older than me, and we always did extracurricular activities together. After she graduated, Ivan and I worked on the yearbook together. He was the editor, and I drew some illustrations for it. We started dating while in university, and we got married in 1997. In 2000, we moved from Mississauga to London, Ontario. We love to travel and see new sights and experience new cultures and foods. See this book's part 2 for more details about how we arrived in London and our past travels.

In 2010, after being married for thirteen years, my husband and I found out we were pregnant. We were so happy for this very special event. It wasn't long after when the "morning sickness" began. The nausea and vomiting happened mostly in the morning, before work. Sometimes I also felt the same during the evenings, after an exhausting day of work.

After I found out we were pregnant, I was very cautious about what I ate and drank. I did not eat anything raw like sushi or seafood. I avoided alcohol, coffee, and tea. I ate as nutritiously as possible while driving very often for work to various locations. I could only tolerate french fries without salt. After I saw the first ultrasound of our baby, eggs repulsed me.

I really enjoyed my work, even though each day had its own share of new stresses and problems. I enjoyed solving problems and finding solutions to complex issues. In my position as a construction and development procurement manager, I had to balance a lot of expectations, both internal (from my manager and our client group, always under pressure to turn around activity in a short time) and external (from bodies like the provincial government, our gaming regulators, consultants, service providers, and taxpayers). My position was an exciting and challenging one because it blended my past experiences as a construction project manager, facilities manager, and operations manager with other companies.

Procuring or buying the services of architects, engineers, contractors, and maintenance service providers happens at the start of a project or initiative, and selecting the right firm can be very challenging. The criteria of being open, fair, and transparent in a public sector environment and in the context of finding reliable, trustworthy, and financially stable construction firms were often more challenging to meet than would appear to the general tax-paying public.

My hands-on experience in the construction field was beneficial to my team and department. Since I had literally "walked in the shoes" of my internal client groups, I could understand and appreciate their challenges. We often travelled to our work sites to gain a better understanding of what purchase was needed. While construction or renovation of a site was going on, I did not mind wearing my construction boots and stepping in the wet mud and dirty drywall dust to take measurements for the furniture, fixtures, and equipment my staff would purchase for the project. My staff and I naturally walked in our client's shoes, to show that "we got it" (i.e., we clearly understood their specific needs).

I enjoyed the combination and balance of office work and on-site construction work. Knowing what my client wanted and showing them in person that my team was committed and dedicated to getting them the right product and solution helped us to be successful.

2. Pregnancy Announcement

On Thanksgiving 2010, Ivan and I announced to our parents first that we were going to have a baby. Then we told the rest of our family. At our family meal, Ivan prayed for "Aunty Lin and baby." His brothers and their wives were in shock, and his brother Colin, who has seven children, said, "What? What did you say? Did you just say you're having a baby? Are you both joking?" Our siblings, in-laws, nieces, and nephews were very excited. My nieces and nephews are very close to "Uncle Ivan." They love his playful nature, even though he often acts very seriously.

We had both our families write down the expected sex, weight, name, and date and time of birth of our baby. Everyone was very excited to give us their guesses. Two people guessed the sex as female but suggested male names.

Ivan guessed that our baby would be a girl, but I thought we would have a boy. So we both shared the task of finding a girl's name and a boy's name. We discussed several, and Ivan thought of *Genevieve*. Sainte Geneviève is the patron saint of Paris, France. The name *Genevieve* has Celtic roots, and we've both travelled to Ireland, Scotland, and England. We both have an affinity for those countries, and we like Celtic music and dance too. I love Paris and have very fond memories of my trips there. It was a good option, and we agreed that our baby girl would be named Genevieve. I didn't have a boy's name to suggest, although I liked the name *Andrew*. We both went to St. Andrew's Church when we lived in Rexdale, Ontario, and St. Andrew was the first apostle Jesus Christ chose.

3. FROM JOY TO DESPAIR

OUR ROLLER-COASTER RIDE BEGAN THE DAY AFTER OUR HAPPY ANNOUNCEMENT to our families. We dropped from an extreme high of joy and happiness to the depths of despair when I learned that one of my five sisters was admitted to a Toronto hospital for attempted suicide. This sister was five years older than me.

I was driving on the highway from London back to Toronto when I received the call. I immediately called my director at work to advise of the urgent medical emergency that I needed to take care of. We were supposed to attend an awards ceremony at a prestigious hotel in downtown Toronto that evening.

When I arrived at the hospital, my sister was about to be discharged. She seemed very calm to me, but I knew she still needed help. I took her back to her house and stayed with her.

In the evening, my sister went to use the washroom. After a while, I grew concerned. When I knocked on the washroom door, there was no answer. I started getting more worried as I continued to knock on the door. Some people who lived with her knew something was wrong too. I feared the worst.

We discovered that my sister had escaped out of the washroom window. I frantically ran out the door and down the street to look for her. She lived on Avenue Road, a major road in Toronto that continues north from Yonge Street. It was already dark outside, and I vividly remember vehicle lights coming toward me. The people with whom my sister lived ran out with me to track her down.

I was a wreck, crying hysterically in the middle of Avenue Road. I called my husband, who was working in Toronto that day. Ivan drove up Avenue Road in his car just as my sister reappeared. One of the people she knew had found her.

My sister saw how distraught I looked. Ivan immediately told me to calm down and breathe slowly so that I could catch my breath. He was very worried about our baby's condition in my frantic and panicked state.

We then returned to my sister's house. She was clearly still very upset. She threatened again to kill herself because she didn't see any hope or future ahead of her. Someone in the house contacted the police, who came to the house and sent my sister by ambulance to a different hospital in downtown Toronto. Ivan and I followed the ambulance in our own cars.

As expected, we waited and waited in the emergency room for her to be assessed. Eventually the doctor recommended that she be moved to and assessed by the Centre for Addiction and Mental Health (CAMH). We waited again for the ambulance to move her down the street. It was an extremely tiring, stressful, and emotionally draining day that ended at around 5:30 the next morning.

Ivan had already booked a hotel in downtown Toronto for his work. The hotel was fortunately within walking distance from the hospital. After my sister was settled in at CAMH, Ivan and I, completely physically and mentally exhausted, went to the hotel to rest.

The next day, a long and stressful journey began to help my sister to see reality and understand the depths of her despair that caused her to attempt suicide. My father-in-law lent me an image of Our Lady of Guadalupe's face. He said that I should pray to Our Lady and ask my sister to pray to Her too. I brought Our Lady's image to CAMH for my sister and prayed the rosary with her. Whenever I was in Toronto for work, I visited my sister at the hospital.

My sister was eventually released from CAMH in late November 2010. Up to the night before her discharge, the release plan was for her to begin anew in London with Ivan and me. We had a spare room in our house, and we thought London was a more "civil" city compared to the hustle and bustle of Toronto. However, the next day she told her doctor that she would live in Mississauga, in our parents' home. Over the course of her stay at the hospital we had slowly moved her clothes and work stuff from her home in Toronto to our home in London. We then had to think about how to get these things back to her in Mississauga. Later my sister drove herself to London, got her things, and drove back to Mississauga.

4. EMERGENCY HOSPITAL VISIT IN TORONTO

ON DECEMBER 8, 2010, I WAS AGAIN IN TORONTO FOR MY WORK. IVAN WAS returning from doing a project in Ottawa and stopped in Toronto for his work.

That morning, I woke up feeling queasy and unwell. I told my office colleague that I felt nauseous and my head hurt a lot. She told another colleague, who handled emergencies for the staff. She in turn suggested that I lie down in the first aid room. I said it wasn't necessary, but soon I was on my back in the first aid room bed.

A security officer took my blood pressure and said that it was too high or too low (I can't clearly recall). Before I knew it, I was being put on a stretcher and heading in an ambulance to nearby North York General Hospital (NYGH). My good friend and colleague contacted Ivan. He arrived at NYGH before my ambulance. Another manager brought my purse with my health card and took my colleague back to the office when he saw that Ivan was with me.

Ivan had worked with NYGH on several significant projects. For example, he helped the staff improve hand-hygiene compliance. He was very familiar with the staff in the emergency area and was able to connect with them before my ambulance arrived. One of the Emergency Management Services (EMS) staff said to me, "Wow—you must know somebody in this hospital." At that moment, I was in too much pain to say that my husband knew several people in the NYGH organization, including the CEO (Chief Executive Officer) and emergency room staff.

I explained to Ivan, the nurses, and the doctors that I just felt nauseous and had a bad headache. I was discharged that evening with a headache, and no medication was prescribed, since I was pregnant. No ultrasound scans or magnetic resonance imaging (MRI) scans were done. I was very fortunate because if a scan had revealed something abnormal in my brain, my baby would have only been six months old. She possibly would have been severely under-developed for delivery and survival.

At that moment, we only knew that we had survived another hospital event without much fuss or hassle. Thank God that He is always watching over us, His beloved children.

December 8 was the Feast of Our Mother Mary's Immaculate Conception. This feast day is significant in the Roman Catholic Church because it recognized the Mother of Jesus as "free of sin at conception." It was our Lord's divine will that Our Mother Mary was immaculately conceived. In retrospect, I firmly believe that Our Mother Mary (I'll also refer to Her as "Our Lady") was looking over Ivan, our baby and me on Her special feast day. She knew the plan of her son Jesus for our family. She made sure no invasive tests were performed at NYGH.

5. Emergency Hospital Visits in London

In late January 2011, I started to understand what "baby brain" meant. I was having difficulty remembering names and felt at a loss for words. My colleagues at work told me not to worry. They said, "You're just having 'baby brain.'"

On February 1, 2011, I was eight months pregnant and went to work in London as usual. I began to feel dizzy and nauseous at work and asked my staff to help me get to the hospital. They could tell that I needed immediate medical attention. Two colleagues took me to St. Joseph Hospital's emergency room. In the car, I phoned one of my internal clients on a key project that I was working on. I told him that I would call back after my hospital visit. However, due to the events that unfolded, I never called him back.

One of my staff asked another manager in our Toronto office to contact my husband, who was working in Toronto that day. Ivan immediately left his meetings and drove to London. When he arrived at the hospital, my two colleagues returned to work. I felt hungry, and Ivan asked a nurse to find me something to eat. I recall eating a tasteless cucumber sandwich. I had no contractions or immediate signs of birth, and after monitoring my belly, they discharged me to go home.

Two days later, on Thursday, February 3, Ivan prepared a delicious Chinese New Year dinner with several courses. Although he is not Chinese, he learned the Chinese traditions that we still maintain as Canadian citizens. Typically, Chinese New Year is celebrated with lots of fanfare and noise to ring in the new year and to bid the previous year goodbye. But I couldn't keep anything down in my stomach. I was incoherent and throwing up a lot. Ivan decided to take me back to St. Joseph's emergency. He tried to get the nurses to see me, explaining that I was not eating and was worried that it was affecting our baby's life.

Eventually the emergency staff released me, saying that I probably had the flu and needed to rehydrate and drink more liquids. Ivan returned home very disappointed because he knew I didn't have a flu. The hospital staff clearly did not "get it" at the time.

When I was discharged, I looked worse than before I entered the hospital. Ivan recalled some nurses wondering why I was being discharged when clearly I did not look well at all. The discharge nurses were apparently ambivalent to my condition, and Ivan was very frustrated that they showed no sense of care.

After this second visit, we were scheduled for an ultrasound at St. Joseph's Hospital on Monday, February 7. I became less coherent and did not make any sense. When Ivan asked me for my health card, I gave him a piece of paper and insisted that it was my health card. I continued to throw up more frequently until I emptied everything in my stomach and threw up bile. As Ivan washed and dried bedsheets, pillows, pillowcases, the couch, and the carpet, I threw up again. It was exhausting for him to lug me up and down our stairs, in and out of the car, to the hospital and back. This is where our marriage vows of "in sickness and in health" were fully demonstrated. Every time I threw up, Ivan cleaned up, so that I could throw up again.

He even went out to buy Gravol to control my nausea. I didn't realize it until a few months later when I saw a partial package of Gravol in our medicine drawer. I asked him when we bought it, and he looked at me with surprise and said, "When you were so sick, before I took you back to the hospital." Sadly, I didn't even remember that event.

On Monday, February 7, we were back at St. Joseph's Hospital for the third time. An astute nurse noticed that I was not coherent and could not remember the date after I had just been told it. She probed further and noticed that my pupils were not dilating. She thought that my problem was possibly neurologically related. Ivan recollects that she asked me to recall details of the day before, and I told her about events from high school. She asked me the date; I told her it was October 14, 1984. I'm not even sure why I chose that date. This nurse truly "got it." She could tell that I needed immediate attention, and she convinced the doctor that I did not have the flu.

The doctor examined me and said that I needed to be sent to University Hospital for further tests. I was rushed there by ambulance for an emergency MRI. St. Joseph's is approximately three kilometres south of University Hospital. The hospital porters yelled down the hallways to clear a path for my bed so I could go to the emergency room at University Hospital without delay. Several calls were made between the two hospitals to secure an immediate MRI scan for me. There were three other pregnancy-related emergencies that same day. The hospital staff were extremely vigilant.

After the MRI scan of my brain, the doctors asked to talk to Ivan, who had been anxiously wondering what they had found. After midnight, the doctors and surgeons at University Hospital advised Ivan that I had a tumour in my brain. They could not determine what type of growth was in my skull, but they could tell that it was rather large. They recommended immediate surgery to relieve the pressure in my head. Originally they suspected that I had a meningioma (a tumour on the outer protective layer of tissue surrounding the brain).

Ivan contacted my mother and his parents and asked his parents to make arrangements to bring my mom to London. He told them it was urgent that they come. Our families are primarily in the Mississauga, Ontario, area (approximately 180 kilometres away from London).

Ivan met with the medical and surgical teams and discussed two operations, the brain surgery and the delivery of our baby. He insisted that there be only one point of contact from the medical team back to him. He wanted the communication lines to be clear. The medical team appreciated his concerns and was diligent to follow up. Ivan discussed the sequence, risks, and benefits of the brain surgery and delivery of our baby. He later told me that when he added up all the percentages of things that could have gone wrong, I had a greater than 85 percent chance of death or severe unrecoverable injury.

Given all the potential risks and complications, Ivan gave permission to the medical and surgical team to begin with a Caesarean section

(C-section) so our baby could be born first. After the C-section, the doctors could administer drugs to me so that I could undergo my brain surgery or craniotomy. Ivan also had to sign off permission for me to have a blood transfusion if necessary.

One obvious complication was delivering our baby. I was at University Hospital, which did not have any obstetrical care. St. Joseph's Hospital had a birthing centre and assessment area.

The neurologists contacted my obstetrician at St. Joseph's Hospital. The risks and benefits of delivering our baby in a hospital that had no obstetrical care were cautiously considered. Ultimately, it was decided that the safest route was to put all the equipment, tools, materials, etc., into an ambulance and send the staff from St. Joseph's Hospital to University Hospital. A special city-wide team was dispatched. This special medical team took care of such emergencies and unique situations.

My obstetrician was scheduled to begin vacation that day. She delayed her departure because she knew that I would be confident in her ability to safely deliver our baby. Our baby was technically only eight months old. Over the course of my pregnancy, I had had several ultrasounds. Some ultrasounds were repeated so that the beating heart of our fetus could be seen on the screen. In one ultrasound, we saw our baby playing and yawning. It was so wonderful and heart-warming to see, tears welled up in my eyes.

Ivan's family began to arrive in London. Ivan's older brother (Colin) wisely asked him if he wanted our church pastor to administer last rites to me. The likelihood of death during the surgeries was high at the time. Ivan agreed and directed Colin to contact our pastor. He arrived at the hospital and gave me my last rites before I went in for my surgeries.

It was a very stressful and tiring time for Ivan because he had to make quick but informed decisions on my behalf. He had to constantly think about whether his thoughts were aligned with what I'd want. Since I was unconscious, he was completely alone to make such critical life-or-death decisions. After I regained consciousness, I assured Ivan that he had made the right choices for our baby and me as he had saved our lives.

Urgent Prayers Needed

Prayer is putting oneself in the hands of God.
—Mother Teresa of Calcutta (1910–1997)

In the meantime, the University Hospital staff gave Ivan and our families a special room to meet and pray in. Our families prayed for a safe delivery of our baby by saying the Divine Mercy Chaplet.[1]

Our baby, Genevieve, was delivered at 3:13 p.m. on February 8th, 2011. This time is exceptionally significant because three o'clock is the "Hour of Great Mercy," recalling the time of Jesus' death on the cross.

Jesus appeared to St. Faustina and said, as she wrote in her diary, "for at that moment mercy was opened wide for every soul. In this hour you can obtain everything for yourself and for others for the asking."[2] Jesus indeed had mercy on all of us that miraculous day in February.

After the Divine Mercy Chaplet had been said for the ninth time (completing the nine-hour novena), the head neurosurgeon came to Ivan and explained that the craniotomy operation was successful and that I was now in recovery in the intensive care unit (ICU). It was a great relief knowing that all of the serious risks and complications of the two surgeries did not compromise the successful outcome.

I firmly believe that Jesus heard all of the prayers that had been raised up to Him. He saved our little baby and me from any trauma, problems, or health concerns.

---

1 For more information, see "The Chaplet of the Divine Mercy," The Divine Mercy, Marian Fathers of the Immaculate Conception of the B.V.M., www.thedivine-mercy.org/message/devotions/praythechaplet.php.

2 Seraphim Michalenko et al., *The Divine Mercy: Message and Devotion: With Selected Prayers from the Diary of St. Maria Faustina Kowalska*, rev. ed. (Stockbridge, Massachusetts: Marian Press, 2001), 72.

6. After Surgeries

Genevieve was transported by ambulance back to St. Joseph's Hospital. Ivan followed in his own car. While Genevieve and I were hospitalized, Ivan went back and forth between the two hospitals. He finally got rest after I awoke and regained consciousness and clarity.

After my brain operation, I was moved to the ICU to recover. Ivan's father brought the image of Our Lady of Guadalupe and told Ivan to put it in my room. Many precautions were taken because, I believe, Ivan put the "fear of God" into the surgeons. Ivan had done many improvement projects in several hospitals and knew how to dialogue with the medical team. They were extra-vigilant and careful with my operations and after-care.

When I started to regain consciousness, I saw a framed image of Our Lady of Guadalupe's face by my bedside. With the little strength I had in my voice, I told the nurse, "That's my father-in-law's." I knew it well because it was the same image he had given to me when my sister was at CAMH.

The nurse asked me, "What did you say?"

I repeated, "That's my father-in-law's."

I did not speak clearly enough and was not very coherent, and she thought that I was talking nonsense and possibly the brain surgery had gone very wrong.

She must have thought, "Why is this patient calling a woman's face her father-in-law?"

Later on when I saw Ivan, I asked him why his father's image of Our Lady was in my hospital room. He explained that the MRI scan of my brain had shown a very large abnormality in my skull, and the doctors told him about the risks of operating on my brain while I was eight months pregnant. Our Lady of Guadalupe is the "Protectress of the

Unborn." I firmly believe that Our Lady protected Genevieve, who was born one month before her due date.

When I fully regained consciousness, I had a breathing tube up my nose and a catheter for urination. A whole bunch of tubes and things were all around me to monitor my heart rate, pulse, etc.

When I was finally moved from the ICU to my own private room, I wanted to make sense of what had happened. I still did not "get it" myself. When I saw Ivan again, I asked him what happened and the sequence of events that led to me being at University Hospital. I said, "But we were supposed to deliver our baby at St. Joseph's Hospital in central London. What happened?" Each time I tried to process the information, I asked Ivan for more information about what had happened. He patiently explained the events over and over again. I was still in utter shock!

I found out from Ivan that his parents had come from Mississauga and were taking care of Genevieve for us. He brought his father's image of Our Lady of Guadalupe to my room so that Our Lady could "watch over" me.

I also asked Ivan about the clicking sound that I kept hearing. He looked around everywhere in my hospital room to try to stop the sound. He said he could not hear it to stop it. He thought it was the large round clock hanging on the wall. I continued to hear the annoying clicking noise; I finally let the issue go. Ivan did not hear the sound anywhere.

The nurses from St. Joseph's Hospital and University Hospital helped me to get settled in my room on the 7th floor at University Hospital. I recall the first St. Joseph's nurse cleaning me with a wet towel. She stayed awake in my room. If Genevieve had been born at St. Joseph's Hospital, there would have been many staff to attend to me and Genevieve. Since I had a Caesarean section and Genevieve was also considered a preterm baby, the St. Joseph's Hospital nurses stayed in my room for about two days.

When the nurses changed shifts, another nurse from St. Joseph's health care team gave me a breast milk pumping device and showed me how to use it. It took some time for milk to flow from my breasts. I was very happy when milk started to flow, and I had the neuro-nurse refrigerate it right away. The nurses were happy to oblige. A few days later, I found out from my neuro-oncologist that I shouldn't breastfeed my baby. All the medication that was administered to me during and after surgery would be passed on in my breast milk to Genevieve, who was too young to tolerate it. It was a huge disappointment for Ivan and me. The St. Joseph's Hospital nurses were still very helpful, friendly and knowledgeable.

Even though Genevieve was born preterm, she was a healthy 5 pounds 2 ounces at birth. She had a full head of hair. Many people asked if I had heartburn or ate a lot of pork during pregnancy. I could tolerate very plain food and did not eat anything rich or spicy. Genevieve's fingernails were ready for trimming when I first saw her, the day after she was born. She was bundled heavily; it was windy and cold outside. One of the nurses at St. Joseph's Hospital told Ivan that Genevieve was the youngest "outpatient" they had ever had.

The staff at University Hospital knew that I had just given birth and put a little bassinette in my room. I was so excited to see Genevieve that I started cleaning up my room and arranging my flowers and cards. I also rolled the bassinette so that it was beside my bed.

When Ivan and the nurses heard that I was moving things around, they scolded me. I shouldn't have been moving heavy bags of sheets or the bassinette (though it was on wheels).

They knew that I could barely walk when I gained consciousness. It was excruciatingly painful to move my legs, and I had to hold on to the wall. When I was pregnant, I had pain from sciatica. This time, the pain was in both my legs and buttocks. Walking was very, very time consuming and terribly painful. When I looked at myself in the mirror, I looked like an "elegant boxer": I had blue-black bruises around my eyes and a big hair updo so the surgeons could get into my skull.

Eventually I had several lines removed from me. I could become more mobile and independent. After a breathing tube, massaging leg braces, blood pressure monitors and a catheter were removed, I felt so free—until I tried to walk. I had to use a commode (a portable toilet seat on wheels) to move myself around the hospital room. I used it like an elderly person uses a walker to be mobile. It was not a pleasant experience, to say the least. The nurses gave me painkillers like Tylenol 3 to handle the pain. I resisted at first, but I had to take them to control the severe pain in my legs and lower back.

Two days after my surgeries, I went back for another MRI scan to see how much of the tumour was removed. I recall the room being extremely cold and being told to lie completely still.

Seven days after surgery, seeing all my leg and back pain, the neurosurgeon ordered another MRI of my lumbar spine. I was rolled into the MRI machine, and after a few minutes, the radiology technician wheeled me out of the machine and asked if I knew that I had just delivered a baby. I guess the doctors did not indicate that I just had a baby on the MRI requisition.

It seemed like every moment of the day was spent seeing medical staff:

- The nurses took my temperature and blood pressure every four hours, even during my "rest/sleep" time.
- The hospital's occupational therapist (OT) visited often to check on my recovery. She kept telling me to get well fast. She said that I could catch something that I didn't want to have. I knew from Ivan that the OT was referring to other patients passing on bacteria like MRSA (methicillin-resistant staphylococcus aureus, which is bacteria resistant to antibiotics) or C-difficile (clostridium difficile, which is a bacterium that causes mild to severe diarrhea and intestinal conditions).
- The hospital's physiotherapist (PT) also visited me frequently to check on my progress. Since my legs were virtually immobile, she recommended some exercises.
- My neurosurgeon and sometimes his students also visited often to see how I was healing. After hearing I couldn't walk well after surgery, the neurosurgeon ordered another MRI.
- My obstetrician's "stand-in" while she was on vacation also paid me a visit. The stand-in doctor did a quick check and was on her way.

- Another neurosurgeon visited me, and I was not in the mood for more visitors that day until he told me who he was; he was one of the neurosurgeons who had operated on my tumour. I was able to personally thank him for operating on me.

When I had a fever, the neurosurgeon recommended that I have an ultrasound to rule out any problems from my C-section. A porter and nurse lifted me from my sheets and rolled me onto a board. The board was painfully hard on my back. I drank so much water so the ultrasound would scan clearly that as soon as I was put on the board, I felt like I needed to pee.

When I arrived at the ultrasound exam room, the radiology technician got an urgent page and had to leave. I didn't even have time to say, "I desperately need to pee." I hobbled back onto the bed and managed to push myself out of the exam room and into the hallway. I called down the hallway for help; no one passed by. I saw a washroom sign, jumped painfully off the gurney, and held on to the wall like a spider as I dragged my legs to move to the washroom. I could not hold my pee any longer. As soon as I sat down on the toilet, it was *total relief*. Ahhhh!

I finished and slowly got up and managed to wash my hands. I hailed someone to help me get a porter to take me back to my room. A porter finally came back for me and wheeled me back. Later I had to go through the agony again to refill my bladder so that the ultrasound could be done.

I was at University Hospital for a total of ten days. My parents-in-law visited me. My nephew, who is also my godchild, visited too. He didn't know what to say or do. I found out that my mom and two of my sisters from Mississauga visited the hospital before my surgeries. My brother and his kids from the U.S.A. visited after I regained consciousness. They saw me at University Hospital and visited Genevieve at St. Joseph's Hospital. One of my nieces, who was studying at the university, walked over to visit me. My eldest sister and family in the U.S.A. and colleagues from work sent beautiful flowers and cards.

The hospital environment is a little scary. Some people stayed away, feeling a little numb or too scared to visit. Some didn't know what to say, so they said nothing. Cancer seems so common, and we often hear of deaths due to it. Maybe some felt that they could catch cancer by being with someone who's so sick. Maybe some thought that if they didn't see me in the hospital, they could deny that I was gravely ill. Although I had several visitors, I felt alienated.

7. A Surprise Visit

When my obstetrician came back from vacation, she remembered to visit me at University Hospital. I thanked her for doing my surgery even though she was about to leave on vacation. She really "got it" and fully understood what I was going through.

She recommended that I not breastfeed my baby. She also advised me that I could not be the primary caregiver for my baby. I said my parents-in-law from Mississauga were helping us in the short term. For the long term, we were looking for a live-in nanny or caregiver. She said that would be a good idea, and she had a nanny herself.

I was very happy that she visited me to follow up on my healing. I needed to talk. She was very understanding and took time to listen to my worries about my brain tumour. She said I was very lucky that I had not been driving a vehicle when I lost consciousness.

I also talked with my obstetrician about my concern about postpartum depression. I had previously told her about depression being prevalent in my family. One of my sisters had also warned Ivan to watch me, especially on the third day after childbirth; she had experienced postpartum depression after all of her children were born, although it did not last long, compared to other women. Fortunately for me, postpartum depression did not occur.

My obstetrician advised me to focus on getting better and seeing Genevieve grow up. She also advised that the staples on my abdomen could be removed by the neuro-nurse after a few more days, and her office would schedule a follow-up appointment in six weeks. She totally "got it" and understood. She knew that I had many things to keep in mind. Her office would set up the appointment so I didn't have to worry about calling them.

8. My "Aha" Moment

My recovery in the hospital seemed very long. I could only look up at the clock ticking away and the blank white ceiling. Ivan said that it was good to get to know the nurses, cleaners and other hospital staff. It was good advice; otherwise it would have felt very awkward to have "strangers" coming into my room.

I asked Ivan to bring from home my rosary, my little wooden icon image of Our Lady holding the infant Jesus, and one of St. Anthony. One of the hospital cleaners saw these things in my room and said, "Oh, a Catholic, eh?" I proudly said, "Yes." He was a friendly cleaner from St. Mary's Parish in London, and he told me about his Scottish background. Ivan and I have travelled to Scotland, so it was easy conversation.

While resting in my hospital bed, I tried to think of what could have caused my brain tumour:

- Maybe I should have listened more to my mother when she told me not to go out with wet hair in the mornings? I remember going to university when my hair was still wet and sitting on a shuttle bus from Mississauga to the downtown Toronto campus and my hair freezing on the window. It was four years of one-hour journeys each way to get to school and back home.
- Maybe I studied too hard at school?
- Maybe I had too many "all-nighters" during school?
- Maybe I drank too much cold black coffee when I was very young (under seven years old)?
- Maybe it was caused by my scar when I fell at seven years old and got stitches on my right side of my head? (But my tumour was on the left side.)

- Maybe when I drove to various sites for work, I used the cellphone too much on my left ear? I remember having a terrible headache after using the Bluetooth device (so I could be hands-free).
- Maybe I drank too much water from plastic bottles while travelling for work?
- Maybe...maybe...maybe... There were many scenarios that came to my mind.

I found it very hard to pray, even though I held the rosary in my hand. One night I decided to try to say the rosary, and I found myself wallowing in self-pity. In a large family of seven children, I was the sixth child and sixth daughter. My only brother was born after me. I felt I was always a neutral person in my family, helping my siblings and nieces when they were in need. Ivan and I enjoyed being the good and playful "uncle and aunt." So when I started to think about all the problems I averted in my family, like helping my sister avoid suicide, I asked God, "Why me?... Why me?" The thought then entered my mind that Jesus and Mother Mary too were innocent and loving people but yet we unjustly crucified Jesus for all His teachings on love, mercy and forgiveness. How awful for a mother to witness Her innocent son being whipped and crucified!

I thought about Jesus praying in the Garden of Gethsemane on the night He was betrayed, the night before His crucifixion. He prayed to Our Father in heaven to ask Him to take the cup of suffering away. But then He said, "not my will but yours be done" (Luke 22:42). Jesus knew the suffering that He would endure but yet He asked for God's will to be done. I realized there and then, in my hospital room, that my recovery from surgeries was insignificant compared to the suffering Jesus and His Mother went through. Jesus was a good person. He had only good intentions for everyone.

Jesus was perfectly innocent, but he was subjected to brutal torture. I had to bear needles in my arms, but Jesus had to bear the piercing of large nails in His hands and feet and the searing pain while hanging on a cross. I have a permanent scar on my head that stretches from the top of one ear to the top of the other ear like a hairband. Jesus had a crown of thorns piercing His head. He also had a lance speared into His side. I cannot imagine the pain and suffering that Jesus endured for us.

I eventually "got it." I thought to myself, *Aha!* I was complaining to Jesus, who probably made me realize that suffering is a natural part of life. I needed to suffer to truly appreciate and experience life in its fullness. I've heard before that there is "no resurrection without a crucifixion." It was very clear to me that my journey would be one of suffering but that there would be a light at the end of the tunnel.

The next time I saw Ivan, I told him my "revelation." He nodded his head and told me not to worry. Ivan reassured me that he would always be with me through whatever we had to go through. He was my true guardian angel on earth.

I told Ivan that this brain tumour journey was ours to bear together. I really needed his help to keep my sanity in check. I told him that I had no regrets in life. We had travelled a lot, and I still had a list of places that I wanted to see, but if I didn't get to them, I wasn't going to be too upset. I had had a good and active life. We also finally had a baby, and that was everything that we had always hoped for as a couple.

I later read in Henri Nouwen's book *Can You Drink The Cup?*, "We can choose to drink the cup of our life with the deep conviction that by drinking it we will find our true freedom. Thus, we will discover that the cup of sorrow and joy we are drinking is the cup of salvation."[3] God Almighty knows and understands the big picture; we, His children, only have a narrow view of our lives until He gives us the challenge of suffering to offer us the opportunity to open our eyes widely.

I also thought about meeting the first female Canadian astronaut, Dr. Roberta Bondar. I worked closely with her for a team meeting held in Sault Ste. Marie in 2008. She was also the first neurologist in space. I thought that maybe God had planned that I would know someone as significant as Dr. Bondar. She has seen the earth from outer space. What a formidable experience! She "got it" when she rocketed out of the earth's atmosphere into space and saw the whole planet—now that's a real world

---

3 Henri J. M. Nouwen, *Can You Drink the Cup?* (Notre Dame: Ave Maria Press, 1996), 90.

view! I recall her saying how short our lives are compared to the age of the earth and the whole universe.

I was convinced that everyone we meet in life is not a coincidence and that God's plans are never the same as our plans. God is the Master Planner in life, and we only see a small part of the big picture. We need to take the time to reflect on our lives and what we've done with them. Cancer has the power to put the brakes on so we have a chance to pause and think about what we've done with our lives and what we still want to do. We have to appreciate the present moment and use it well.

I finally decided that it was time to move on with life. I carried on with the attitude "it is what it is."

9. Visit With Members of My Cancer Care Team

Before Genevieve was discharged from St. Joseph's Hospital, the nurses taught Ivan how to bathe, feed and burp her. She was discharged on February 12 (four days after her birth). I was looking forward to leaving the hospital on Sunday, February 13, but since my legs were still very sore, the neurosurgeon said he could not discharge me yet.

I met my chemotherapy oncologist, who was also a neuro-oncologist, on Saturday, February 12. He was a very pleasant older gentleman carrying a black "doctor's bag."

The relatively large size of the tumour had suggested at first to the surgeons that they were dealing with a tumour on the surface of the brain. However, once the craniotomy began, they knew it was not a meningioma (a growth on the brain surface rather than inside the brain).

The brain tumour was located in my left prefrontal cortex. At its largest dimension, it was 8 cm or the size of an orange. It was interesting that tumours are compared to fruit sizes. I'd heard of brain tumours the size of a lime but not as large as an orange.

Samples of my brain tissue were taken for analysis. My neuro-oncologist said that the results of the pathology were not completed yet. He advised that only two-thirds of my tumour was resected or removed through surgery. The delineation between brain and tumour was hard to define. The surgeons opted to leave the remaining tumour to be safe and not cause irreparable damage or side effects. When the results were known and the pathology report written up, he could then advise on the follow-up treatment and procedures. (See the appendix for images of my brain before and after surgery, figures 4 and 5.)

I continued to focus with a hospital physiotherapist on using my legs more regularly. When I was on pain medications, I walked better, but I didn't want to get "hooked" on them. I recall that when one of my nurses was changing shifts, she told the next nurse, "This patient does not like to take painkillers." I was happy that the nurses finally "got it" and understood my concerns about becoming too dependent on pain medications.

Slowly but surely, I was able to let go of the railing on the hospital hallways. I progressed each day and was able to limp along where there were no railings (for example, past doors). With the hospital physiotherapist monitoring me, I eventually pulled myself one step at a time up the fire exit stairs. It was excruciatingly painful. I wanted to go home to see my baby, so I persisted with practising my walking and climbing up and down the stairs.

My ultrasound results showed that my leg pains were not related to my C-section. My results were clear with no concerns from my neurosurgeon. Once he saw that I was ambulatory, he said that I could be discharged.

The occupational therapist saw me also and said that I was ready to be discharged. She would arrange for the OT from the Community Care Access Centre (CCAC) to do a home visit with me.

The physiotherapist said that she would see if a PT from CCAC could also do a home visit with me to follow up on my leg pains.

The social worker gave me a follow-up contact to meet with the London Regional Cancer Program (LRCP) clinic's social worker. She was very attentive and compassionate to our situation.

When I finally got the okay to discharge from all hospital departments, I got the full release to go home. I was *so* very happy to be going to see Genevieve at home. Ivan had brought her to the hospital to see me, but after a few visits I told him to keep her at home because she was sneezing. I didn't want her to get sick while visiting me in the hospital. Every time Genevieve sneezed, my heart throbbed. Later I found out that I should not have worried; babies often sneeze a lot after birth to expel the mucous out of their noses.

Before I was discharged, Ivan met with the nurse practitioner and got a list of my prescriptions, a list of medications administered to me while in the hospital, and reports from my surgeries. I took the opportunity to ask the nurse practitioner if the clicking sound I heard would stop. She replied, "Yes—eventually the sound will stop. You are still healing. The skull is still merging back together."

I could see that Ivan was surprised to hear the nurse practitioner acknowledge that the clicking sound actually existed. I wasn't imagining the sound at all. It was not the clicking of the large clock in my hospital room. Ivan hadn't understood what noise I was talking about because he couldn't see anything in my room except the clock that would make a clicking sound. I felt frustrated because there was no external or visible "thing" causing the repetitive clicking. I knew that I had to put up with the sound in my head.

The nurse practitioner advised that my neurosurgeon would follow up in six weeks' time. I didn't have to call to set up an appointment.

I was finally discharged from University Hospital on Friday, February 18 (ten days after I had entered). I said goodbye to all my new friends: nurses, cleaners, food delivery people, and others. As I prepared myself to be discharged, I realized as I took off my one-size-fits-all hospital gown and put on my "street clothes" that no one "out there" would know about my two surgeries. No one would really care about or understand what I had been through (mentally, emotionally, spiritually or physically). The reality of the world outside of the hospital niche hit me like a ton of bricks as I slowly sat in a wheelchair.

Ivan pushed me into the elevator, and I clutched my father-in-law's image of Our Lady of Guadalupe's face. A lady in the elevator remarked that she knew of Our Lady of Guadalupe and also believed in her; it made me happy to hear that from a stranger.

10. Finally Going Home

When I finally returned home, I saw my family, who came with my nieces and nephews. It was good to see all of them. I could barely walk to hug them. My head was still throbbing with the strange clicking sound.

While my family was at our house, Ivan's brother and wife came to visit too with their seven kids. The house was full of noise and lots of "sh…sh…shhhhhhhh." Only one loud person did not respect or understand that I had just had my gut cut open to deliver a baby and my skull sawed open to remove a large tumour. This person just did "not get it," even though I kept explaining and asking for quiet. It was very frustrating when the person callously responded, "I cannot help that I am loud."

After our family left, the silence was truly welcomed. It felt good to be sleeping in my own bed and eating food made by Ivan, rather than checking off bland food on a hospital menu.

11. LONG-AWAITED PATHOLOGY RESULTS

In the midst of the sorrows is consolation, in the midst of the darkness is light, in the midst of despair is hope, in the midst of Babylon is a glimpse of Jerusalem, and in the midst of the army of demons is the consoling angel. The cup of sorrow, inconceivable as it seems, is also the cup of joy. Only when we discover this in our own life can we consider drinking it.

—Henri Nouwen[4]

I WAS SCHEDULED TO SEE MY NEURO-ONCOLOGIST ON TUESDAY, FEBRUARY 22, at the London Regional Cancer Program (LRCP) Clinic at Victoria Hospital. This was the third hospital in London that I had visited in a matter of two weeks.

Before we got pregnant, Ivan and I joked that we paid too much for health care and hadn't used the system very much. We didn't even know that not all London hospitals deliver babies and also didn't know of any obstetricians to suggest to our family doctor. After we had Genevieve, we thanked God for the health care we had and didn't complain or joke about it anymore. We certainly need to appreciate what we have instead of criticizing the cost of an essential service like hospitals and accessible health care.

At my appointment, Ivan and I were first greeted by the radiation oncologist's nurse. She was very pleasant, and she talked to me about postpartum depression, which I was fearful of. Fortunately, my mind was so preoccupied that I had no time to be sad or tearful or wallow in self-pity. The nurse really understood and "got it" about postpartum depression. I appreciated her advice and compassion.

4 Nouwen, *Can You Drink the Cup?*, 43.

After the visit with the nurse, we waited to see my radiation oncologist. A young lady entered and introduced herself as a "fellow" to my radiation oncologist, who would follow later on.

It was this fellow who broke the news of my pathology results to us. Ivan and I were anxious to know the results. We were expecting to hear the word "benign." She explained that my pathology results indicated that I had a glioblastoma multiforme tumour of grade four (or in short, GBM IV) in my left prefrontal cortex. She went on to explain that the GBM grade IV indicated a fast-growing malignant tumour. A GBM grade IV tumour was currently an incurable, malignant, life-threatening disease and the most aggressive type of primary brain tumour. It literally was the worst kind of brain tumour. She said the tumour showed characteristics of both a grade III and grade IV tumour. Hence, she said, the oncologists recommended the typical treatment for GBM IV, which was six weeks of radiation simultaneously with chemotherapy. The oncologists also recommended that I start radiation and chemotherapy immediately because of the size of my tumour and its rapid growth.

That was a lot of information to take in at one time. I was so glad that Ivan was there with me to listen to the pathology results. To put it very mildly, Ivan and I were completely overwhelmed with the results.

Although I had had an "Aha" moment while recovering in the hospital, I burst into tears right in front of the fellow and couldn't stop crying. All I could think of was Genevieve, who was only two weeks old. I had to grasp the fact that I indeed had cancer. Many crazy thoughts raced through my mind, like *Why me?* and *How did this happen?* We were both in sheer shock and utter disbelief.

The Canadian Cancer Society defines cancer as follows:

Cancer is a disease that starts in our cells. Our bodies are made up of millions of cells, grouped together to form tissues and organs such as muscles and bones, the lungs and the liver. Genes inside each cell order it to grow, work, reproduce and die. Normally, our cells obey these orders and we remain healthy. But sometimes the instructions get mixed up, causing the cells to form lumps or tumours, or spread through the bloodstream and lymphatic system to other parts of the body.

Tumours can be either benign (non-cancerous) or malignant (cancerous). Benign tumour cells stay in one place in the body and are not usually life-threatening. Malignant tumour cells are able to invade nearby tissues and spread to other parts of the body.[5]

I asked the fellow, "What is the typical lifespan of someone diagnosed with GBM IV?"

She hesitated to respond. Then she replied, "Do you really want to know?"

I replied, "Yes. I want to know, so that I am prepared."

She responded cautiously. I heard her say, "Everyone's brain tumour and effects of radiation and chemotherapy will be different although the diagnosis is GBM IV. Typically the lifespan will vary from nine to twelve months; it may be one year or at most about fifteen months." She cautioned again that all patients' lifespan will vary based on different factors like age, overall health, sex, location of tumour, size of tumour, attitude, and so on.

When I heard the short time frame, I cried again. I thought in that moment, *I won't even see Genevieve go to kindergarten or graduate or colour with her.*

The fellow wisely saw that Ivan and I were very distraught and offered to give us some privacy and time to digest the pathology results. When she left the exam room, Ivan and I hugged each other and said, "How is this possible? A tumour of the worst kind? How? Why? When?" We understood together that our combined strength and faith would help us through the difficult cancer journey ahead of us.

Lots of questions raced through our minds. The fellow had reviewed the treatment protocol with us before she left us to be alone. Ivan was far more composed than I was. He thought that we needed to call our church pastor right there in the LRCP private room and ask if he could baptize Genevieve as soon as possible, before I started my daily chemotherapy and radiation treatments.

---

5 "What is Cancer?" Canadian Cancer Society, http://www.cancer.ca/en/cancer-information/cancer-101/what-is-cancer/?region=sk.

Our pastor had generously given Ivan his cellphone number. He was accessible to us at any time. We decided that the baptism would have to happen that very weekend, on Saturday, which was four days away. It would give enough time for out-of-town family and friends to join in Genevieve's baptism. The pastor was extremely accommodating and said, "Whatever will work for you and Lin-Pei. I am here." (Part 2 describes Genevieve's baptism day.)

After we had settled the baptism date, the fellow returned to the room and asked if we had any concerns or questions. I was worried about taking anything radioactive as part of my radiation treatment. She consoled me by saying that my kind of radiation did not involve anything radioactive. I felt better because I knew I could still hold Genevieve to feed her and cuddle her to sleep. She informed me that I needed to get a mask prepared by that Friday (three days later).

The radiation oncologist then joined us in the room. He also asked if we had questions. He repeated what the fellow had already said to us. He then said our follow-ups would be with her.

We did not see the neuro-oncologist that day. We continued to bitterly sob, but we realized together in the LRCP room that "it is what it is," and we left shortly thereafter.

We later learned from the Brain Tumour Foundation of Canada website that there are over 120 different types of brain tumours and that treatments vary and efficacy would be complicated to understand. Every day twenty-seven Canadians are diagnosed with a brain tumour. Currently, 55,000 Canadians are surviving with a brain tumour. Primary brain tumours originate in the brain and occur in eight out of 100,000 people. Non-primary brain tumours originate or metastasize from elsewhere in the body.[6]

I personally had not heard about brain tumours before my situation arose. I knew about other cancers, like breast, lung and prostate cancer. I did some research online and discovered that several significant public

---

6 "Brain Tumour Facts," Brain Tumour Foundation of Canada, http://www.brain-tumour.ca/2494/brain-tumour-facts.

figures, including baseball player Gary Carter, US senator Ted Kennedy, and singer Ethel Merman, endured and died from a GBM brain tumour.[7]

---

7 See "List of people with brain tumors," Wikipedia, https://en.m.wikipedia.org/wiki/List_of_people_with_brain_tumors.

12. MORE APPOINTMENTS AFTER DIAGNOSIS

Visit by the Middlesex–London Health Unit

ON FEBRUARY 24, TWO DAYS AFTER LEARNING ABOUT MY PATHOLOGY RESULTS, we had a scheduled visit at our home from the Middlesex-London Health Unit's nurse. She was assigned to follow up with Genevieve. She weighed Genevieve on a portable scale that she carried with her. Genevieve had gained weight; she was 5 pounds 7 ounces. The nurse was very kind and compassionate and clearly understood our situation. She knew of Our Lady of Guadalupe because of her Latin American background. She realized that we were devout Catholics.

The nurse said that we would qualify for the Healthy Moms, Healthy Babies program. This program involved having a family home visitor come to our home at set intervals to help us with our newborn baby and to give us tips on growth and development. We asked the nurse to help us get a good family home visitor. She replied that she would do her best but could not offer any guarantee or firm commitment.

Furniture Installation

That afternoon, Ivan purchased a bed for his parents so they could stay with us to help with caring for Genevieve. The furniture company delivered the bed, and we paid for them to set it up in Genevieve's bedroom.

Visit from the Occupational Therapist

That same afternoon, the occupational therapist from the Community Care Access Centre visited our house. She wanted to assess our home condition and see how I was functioning. Ivan had bought me a seat for the shower so I wouldn't have to stand for long. I could only pick up things from the floor level with my toes. Ivan joked every time he saw me use my toes to grab something that I needed. He said, "There goes toe dexterity."

The hospital OT and the CCAC OT also reminded me to limit the use of stairs. I didn't realize the number of times during the day that I went up and down the stairs for various reasons. The OT suggested that we buy a different shower seat that would actually fit our narrow tub. The legs of the shower seat we had were not fully flat and secure. We recognized the obvious hazard, but that was the only size seat the store carried. The CCAC OT said she would follow-up again in three weeks and recommended that I also talk to a physiotherapist.

Family Doctor Visit for Genevieve

The next morning, we visited our family doctor for Genevieve's first checkup after birth. Genevieve weighed 5 pounds 10 ounces. The doctor reviewed the immunization schedule with us. Genevieve did not fuss at all and was rewarded with two Winnie the Pooh newborn-size sleepers.

Making a Mask for Radiation

Later that afternoon (three days after we received my pathology results), Ivan and I returned to LRCP to make my mask in readiness for radiation. First I had a computerized tomography (CT) scan of my head while lying on a flat bed. The CT scan was used to take several X-ray images of my head. Then I had a thin sheet of perforated white plastic formed over my face. I could still breathe through the perforations or mesh openings. The sheet was heated with a warm towel and then gently stretched over my face, ears, and neck.

The mask position needed to be accurate so that my head would always be in the same position every time my brain was radiated.

Preparing Our Wills

The following week was again filled with many appointments. Ivan and I had not prepared our wills yet. We thought that we would do it after our baby was born and that we'd have time to find a good lawyer and discuss the essentials.

The only lawyer we knew in London was the real estate lawyer who did our final house purchase transaction. I knew corporate lawyers in Toronto, but they would have been very expensive for a simple will, which we needed sooner rather than later. So we asked our next-door neighbours for a recommendation for a local lawyer. The lawyer they recommended actually came to our house because she "got it" that I was not very mobile with a newborn and the imminent cancer therapy. The lawyer asked many personal questions to get to know Ivan and me. She wanted to understand our situation and why we needed a will drafted so quickly and urgently.

Some of the key points Ivan and I needed to decide and think about included the following:

- Who would be our executor and our back-up person?
- Who would be the legal guardian for our child?
- What were our major assets (financial, physical—house, car, jewellery—and so on)?
- Who would have the right to decide when to "pull the plug" in case of medical emergencies?
- Who would have the power of attorney?

After a few hours, the lawyer knew enough to draft our wills. She was very understanding of our extreme situation. She said she would prepare a draft of our will by the end of the week. We were thrilled because some busy lawyers can take some time to respond to their clients.

Ivan and the lawyer corresponded via email during the week. We kept our wills simple and straightforward. As promised, by the end of the week she had our wills drafted, and she personally came to our house again to witness the signing. We also had to arrange for a supporting witness with us when we signed them.

We felt so relieved after our wills were signed. One very important "deferred" activity was handled smoothly and effectively. We're so thankful to the lawyer and to our next-door neighbours for recommending her.

More Deferred Action Items

The day after the lawyer's initial visit, we had some repairs done to our house that we had deferred. We had two full bathrooms, but when our guest washroom's tub started to overflow and leak into the lower levels, we didn't use that bathroom anymore. We used the shower in our master bedroom. Since my parents-in-law were staying with us, we wanted to make sure both bathrooms were fully functional. Needless to say, we finally had the push needed to get the plumbing repairs in our house done.

Visit from the Physiotherapist

That same day, my CCAC physiotherapist visited our home to see how I was coping after my hospital discharge. She suggested exercises and ways to limit the pain in my legs. She cautioned me about bending into Genevieve's bassinette to pick her up so I did not strain my back. She left me with picture instructions for various exercises and wrote down the number of repetitions and frequency each day. Three weeks later, she followed up.

Visit to My Office in London

On the weekend, Ivan went with me to my office to clear up loose ends. He helped me to gather up my office papers so it looked better organized for the person who would take over my position while I was on maternity leave.

Our Special Evening

On the evening of March 8, 2011, Ivan and I went out for a "date" while his parents looked after Genevieve. It was meant to be a special night of fine dining before my radiation and chemotherapy started the following week. Being very cautious about what I ate, I ordered an entrée with mushrooms and ginger in a light broth. The dish tasted much like the food Ivan cooked for me at home. Based on the description in the menu, I had not expected to see something Ivan made for me at home. I was hoping to eat something different, but I was happy to stay with the "cancer diet regime." We shared a delicious crème brulé dessert together. The dessert was definitely different and not too sweet.

Ivan and I finally had some time together to discuss all that had happened in the past one month since Genevieve was born. We were used to busyness and stress from work and family, but we had never expected or planned for anything like our past month. We managed somehow because our daily jobs had trained and prepared us to stay relatively calm amid extreme stress and chaos.

13. Taking Care of Genevieve

Caring for Our Little Baby

WHILE I WAS RESTING AND RECOVERING IN THE HOSPITAL, IVAN MANAGED WITH the help of his oldest brother to buy the right milk formula for Genevieve. She transitioned well from the hospital's milk to powdered milk formula. It was a relief that Genevieve liked her milk and enjoyed eating.

The scientist-minded Ivan asked all who fed Genevieve to keep a detailed time record of when she drank and the amount. Whenever Genevieve started to make noise or fuss, we'd check the record to determine if she needed to eat or have her diaper changed. The records really helped us to understand Genevieve's noises. In the first six months she rarely cried without any reason. The records were maintained by whoever was feeding her and changing her diapers, and they took the guessing game out of why she might be crying or uncomfortable.

Since I had to undergo chemotherapy and radiation treatments immediately after my pathology results were known, Ivan and I had to urgently make arrangements for the care of our newborn baby.

Very fortunately, Ivan's parents were able and willing to help us care for Genevieve. They live in Mississauga (a two-hour drive from London), and their other two sons live closer to them and were also willing to help us out while Mom and Dad stayed in London. Ivan's parents were very flexible and accommodating because they knew and "got it" that we needed help.

My parents-in-law's mail was picked up regularly, and other routine tasks like snow shovelling, indoor plant watering, making and cancelling doctor's appointments, and so on were taken care of by one of Ivan's two brothers.

My sister-in-law (who has seven kids) came to help me. She said taking care of one newborn was like a "holiday" from her own kids. She was a great "oooo aaaah" mom to Genevieve. She loved hearing her cooing and gurgling and enjoying her milk. She knew Genevieve liked music and being held, and she hummed while she fed her.

My in-laws' extended family members were also very helpful. Some emailed or called Ivan's brothers to see how Ivan, Genevieve and I were doing. The families who had personally encountered cancer in their lives truly understood the challenges we were facing. One uncle provided frozen food (delicious meat pies and vegetable pies) even though we didn't ask for them. He knew that stress can make our brains forget to do the essentials, like taking care of our own bodies.

Members of my immediate family, who are all I have in Canada and the United States, had not personally encountered cancer or the death of a close family member. They only faced cancer through a colleague or someone they read about in the newspaper. Some told me very tragic stories that did not help my mental state. Some suggestions were good, but they did not realize that cancer is unique to an individual. I didn't think that I needed to ask them for help. They wanted me to be very specific or else they wouldn't be able to help. Selfishly, in my mind, I just wanted my own people to be with me. Unfortunately, they saw that I had help from my in-laws, and they didn't want to "interfere." I had offers from my sisters, but they were limited in their ability to help (due to distance from London or other work or family commitments).

My only brother, who lived in the United States at the time, drove up to London with his wife and two young children to see me in the hospital. His little children liked playing with Genevieve and her fuzzy hair.

Every day during my treatments, whenever I could, I would try to feed Genevieve her morning milk before I went to the cancer clinic. I listened to calm baby lullabies, classical music or religious songs because they were soothing for both Genevieve and me. Ivan and I would hum, sing or make up songs for her to encourage her to burp. It was fun to see her burp. She had lots of long spikey hair, and when she didn't yet have control of her neck, her head would bounce and bounce until a burp came out. Sometimes she would burp so loudly that it scared her.

Her eyes would open up wider when she heard the odd sound resonating from her body.

My mother-in-law was very helpful in feeding Genevieve in the middle of the night, at midnight, at 3 a.m. and at 6 a.m. She "got it" because she had been the caregiver for two of her own siblings who had died from cancer. She had always been protective of her children and cared very much for their well-being.

She helped a lot to feed Genevieve and change her diapers. After seeing her struggle to be awake to feed and change my daughter, I asked God to forgive all my ill thoughts about her and her "over-protective" behaviour with her sons. She was naturally, like all mothers, protecting her children. I finally "got it" about motherhood.

My father-in-law liked playing with Genevieve and keeping her distracted with his tickling and shaking her rattles. She liked to giggle and kick when "Papa" played with her.

One day, Ivan asked me if we wanted to celebrate Genevieve's birthday every month on the 8th because we didn't know how long I would live. I thought that was a great idea. I told him that I also wanted to capture every day of her life on camera by taking photos of her. Needless to say, I took many (too many) photos of Genevieve. We also celebrated weekly birthdays. We tried to give Genevieve something on every Tuesday (the actual day she was born) and sang "Happy Birthday." For her birthday surprises she would get things she needed like a soother, teething ring, bib, board books, soothing lullaby music, and so on. After one year, I pulled all Genevieve's birthday photos and created a Winnie the Pooh themed "birthday" photobook album. The album will always be a special keepsake for her and future generations.

In the second year, I only took photos of Genevieve's monthly birthdays. She was now getting tired of hearing "smile—cheese—smile" and "look at the camera." When she looks at her baby photos today, she says, "That's not me!" I have no regrets about taking so many photos. It took a long time to put them into albums, and I enjoyed reviewing them and putting captions on them.

14. Merrymount Children's Centre

Merrymount Children's Centre serves as a crisis centre and is a place where families can get support. Our social worker at the LRCP suggested Merrymount as a place where we could take Genevieve during my cancer treatments. She helped us get the application forms and urged us to check out the facility. The Middlesex-London Health Unit's nurse agreed that Merrymount was a good place to take Genevieve for care while I went for treatments.

We were very fortunate to learn about Merrymount because there are few daycares that handle newborn infants. Parents can take leave from work for up to one year. Most parents keep their babies at home or have a caregiver (friend or family member) take care of them. Typically parents have little need for external daycare when the baby is so young.

On March 11, 2011, Ivan and I met with an intake supervisor at Merrymount. When the supervisor showed us the "infant room" or "play area," we were pleased to see a caregiver on the floor playing with a child who couldn't stand or walk yet.

When the supervisor showed us where the babies would sleep, I could not hold back my tears, knowing that my newborn would be sleeping in another "foreign" bed. It was very painful emotionally as a new mother to know that I couldn't be with my baby girl. I had to restrain myself from outrage about my health. I had to remain as calm as possible. It was very difficult to hold back my tears of regret and anger.

In general, the Merrymount staff were very supportive and co-operative when they knew of our situation. One staff member, who really liked Genevieve, saw us at a local store several years later. She told me that she was always amazed when Ivan and I picked up Genevieve after my chemo and radiation appointments. She was a very compassionate and trustworthy Merrymount caregiver. She understood and could see how tired I was, but yet I wanted to pick up Genevieve.

When we visited with our LRCP social worker sometime later, she was happy to know that Merrymount provided great assistance for us and also relief for Ivan's parents. The social worker commended us on spreading the caregiving workload so that my in-laws would not burn out with all the late night feedings and diaper changes.

At the end of May 2012 we found a full-time daycare for Genevieve and stopped taking her to Merrymount. (See part 2 of this book for more details about Merrymount.)

15. CANCER TREATMENTS

Chemotherapy and Radiation Appointments

ON FRIDAY, MARCH 4, 2011, I HAD MY FIRST APPOINTMENT AT LRCP WITH my neuro-oncologist. A typical appointment began with the nurse measuring my weight, followed by a review of my medications and any issues that I had to discuss with the doctor.

After I was discharged from University Hospital, I started to write all of my appointments in a calendar and all of the questions and answers in a separate book. I also kept a list of my emergency contacts near the telephone, and my chart number too. I wrote a list of questions for each time I would see the chemo or radiation oncologist, and I tried my best to fill in the answers after the appointment. Ivan was consistently with me for every appointment and test. I was grateful that he helped me with my memory gaps.

For example, after the nurse measured my weight, I would forget it. Ivan would remind me of it afterwards so that I could record it accurately in my journal. It was always helpful to have him accompany me to all my appointments. I trusted him wholeheartedly. He has a very clear and organized mind in the midst of stress and chaos, and he also has an excellent memory without needing to take notes.

It's important that someone sound and knowledgeable accompany the patient to appointments. The patient's mind can be cluttered with anxiety or the patient may be feeling too tired to really take in or process the technical and medical information provided by the health care providers.

Being the patient, I needed Ivan to help me interpret what the doctors and nurses were telling me. He was a very patient caregiver, often repeating several times what the doctor had said so that I could finally "get it" myself and accurately note the comments in my book. I brought my book to every oncology and MRI appointment.

Before every appointment (usually as we were driving to the hospital), I said prayers with Ivan to ask Jesus and Mother Mary to help us ask the right questions and to clearly understand the answers. I also carried several prayer cards in my bag. In my hospital bag, I carried my journal, a bottle of water, a throw-up bag, serviettes and hand sanitizer. Using my prayer cards, I prayed to Our Lady of Guadalupe, Our Mother of Perpetual Help and all of the saints and angels and to Blessed Mother Teresa of Calcutta for her intercession with Jesus and His Mother. I also attached to the bag a little blue crystal angel given to me by a parishioner from my Holy Family Parish church. Ivan's brother also gave me a rosary that was touched to St. Pope John Paul II's garment. My father-in-law also gave me a medal of St. Rita. Both the rosary and the medal were also in my hospital bag.

The neuro oncologist described my chemotherapy treatments, which would include daily chemo medications for six weeks. My radiation would also take place during those same six weeks (except on weekends, when the London Regional Cancer Program Clinic was closed). My radiation appointments were scheduled early on during the day after we could make sure Ivan's parents or Merrymount could take care of Genevieve. The oncologists assured us that the radiation appointments were "usually" on schedule. On occasion we encountered delays and even early in-takes, but usually the radiation appointments were on time.

The timing of when I would orally take my chemotherapy pills was dependent on when my radiation appointment was scheduled. A typical daily schedule would be as follows:

- Take anticonvulsant tablets (to control seizures) with breakfast.
- Take acetaminophen to control head pain as needed.
- Four hours before radiation, stop eating food.
- Two hours before radiation, take anti-nausea medication.
- One hour before radiation on weekdays or at mid-morning or mid-afternoon on weekends, take chemotherapy pills.

- Go for radiation on weekdays.
- Take anticonvulsant tablets in the afternoon.
- Take anticonvulsant tablets in the evening.
- Take a multivitamin (discretionary—not required, but I continued with them since they were my daily regime before I was pregnant).

We completed paperwork to be prequalified to receive coverage for the chemotherapy drug. Ivan, on my behalf, called my health care insurance provider. He was bounced from one number to another number in another province. We had naively decided that we would pay for the drug while a decision was being made about my eligibility. At the time, we did not know how expensive the chemotherapy treatment drugs were. (See part 2 of this book for more details about cancer costs.)

The first chemotherapy drug was called temozolomide or Temodal. The neuro-oncologist said that the care routine for me had been prescribed before (for my type and grade of brain tumour). He cautioned that every patient reacted differently to the drugs because of various factors like general health, age, sex, physical and mental activity, location of tumour, type and grade, and so on.

The oncologists were anxious to begin treatments as soon as possible. They feared that my tumour would continue to rapidly grow.

After meeting my neuro-oncologist, I learned,

- A blood test was needed every week (on Mondays) while I was given chemotherapy and radiation.
- Phenytoin (or Dilantin) was an anticonvulsant medication (for managing seizures) and could cause skin irritations or chest rashes.
- Temodal could be taken orally (rather than intravenously) with water or juice but not with milk, and it needed to be taken on an empty stomach. I could not touch the drug with my bare hands. Ivan had to put the drug on the cap of the drug bottle and drop it into my mouth to avoid direct skin contact.

- My starting dose of Temodal would be 120 mg (I told my oncologist that I found it difficult to swallow large pills; he wrote my prescription for smaller sized tablets, so that I would not have difficulty swallowing the medications).
- Side effects of Temodal were nausea; to counteract the nausea, he prescribed antinauseants:
  - Ondansetron, which could cause constipation, for the first to fifth day
  - Stemetil (Prochlorperazine) after the fifth day

The potential side effects of my chemotherapy and radiation regime included,

- a lower blood platelet count, which affects the ability of blood to clot
- a lower white blood cell count, which affects infection control
- typically, one in twenty persons will have blood issues

I was very concerned that my radiation regime might affect my ability to hold my newborn. The oncologist assured me again that my radiation was not using anything radioactive; he advised me to not be concerned.

The oncologist also strongly advised me to use birth control during my treatments. He cautioned that conceiving a baby while I was taking chemotherapy and radiation would be very dangerous for the growth of a fetus.

He also cautioned that radiation might cause skin irritation to my scalp. Unfortunately, the radiation would cause hair loss. The chemotherapy drug would not cause any hair loss.

We would see our radiation oncologist weekly during combined treatments and our neuro-oncologist every two weeks. Two or three weeks after the initial course of radiation and chemotherapy was done, another MRI scan would be done. This MRI scan was important to determine the effectiveness of the combined treatment. After a four-week pause, chemotherapy would likely continue to control the brain tumour growth, depending on the scan results.

At the end of the week, we got approval for coverage of Temodal from my health care insurance provider. We could start treatment without the concern about paying fully for the drug ourselves. We went to the LRCP clinic's pharmacy to get our prescription filled. We gave the pharmacist my prescription, and as usual, she asked for my date of birth and address. When she heard my address, she said she lived very close to that street. After she gave me my medications, we went into another room where she explained when to take the meds and gave me a sheet about the drug.

We then got a chance to ask the pharmacist where exactly she lived. As it turned out, she lived directly across the street from us. Her house was a stone's throw away from our house. She was very kind and pleasant, and she offered her help with my prescriptions whenever I needed it. I felt very relieved. I knew chemo was like poison that would kill both my cancerous and good cells.

At around 5 a.m. on the Sunday before my treatments began, I felt pain on the left side of my face. My lymph glands felt swollen and sore, and I felt sensitivity under my left ear, between my chin and my neck. I recall wrapping myself in a prayer shawl that had been made especially for me. It was a thoughtful gift from a long-time friend whose wife had had breast cancer. The shawl gave me comfort, and I prayed that the swelling would stop. The pain finally subsided before I went to church at 11 a.m.

16. PREPARING FOR CANCER TREATMENTS

I TRIED TO READ AS MUCH AS I COULD ABOUT BRAIN CANCER, RADIATION AND chemotherapy before my treatments started. This included manuals from the Canadian Cancer Society. I took every relevant brochure from the kiosks at the LRCP and read as much as I could absorb in the short period of time before radiation and chemo began. I also read a manual prepared by the Brain Tumour Foundation of Canada that explained my tumour and what the grade meant.

Some cancer patients prefer to be ignorant about what to expect. It may be too scary for them to know the painful truth about what is to come. I, on the other hand, wanted to be as informed as possible about what to expect in order to alleviate my anxiety and worries. I had to constantly remind myself that every person and every tumour location, type and grade are different. Every situation is unique for every individual, and, obviously, outcomes will vary.

I also prepared by making sure that my hospital bag that I took to the LRCP contained all I needed for my radiation and chemo appointments, including my book where I wrote all my questions and answers, my calendar and all my prayer materials.

17. Brain and Cancer Information

THE MATERIALS I READ TO UNDERSTAND MY TUMOUR AND TREATMENTS WERE available free of charge. They included the following:

1. From the Brain Tumour Foundation of Canada:

- *Brain Tumour Patient Resource Handbook, Adult Version*, 5th ed. (2009)

2. From the Canadian Cancer Society:

- *Brain Tumours - Understanding Your Diagnosis* (2008)
- *Chemotherapy—A Guide for People With Cancer* (2004)
- *Eating Well When You Have Cancer—A Guide to Good Nutrition* (2008)
- *Facing Cancer?—We Can Help* (2010)
- *Helpful Hints for the Newly Diagnosed* (2007)
- *Helping Someone with Cancer—What You Can Do* (2004)
- *Living with Advanced Cancer* (2010)
- *Preventing Cancer* (2010)
- *Radiation Therapy—A Guide for People With Cancer* (2005)
- *Seven Steps to Health* (2008)

The information was helpful in managing my anxieties and worries about what I was about to endure in the weeks ahead, and I felt more in control.

18. TREATMENT WEEKS 1, 2 AND 3

I STARTED MY FIRST DAY OF CHEMOTHERAPY AND RADIATION ON MONDAY, March 14, 2011 (three working days after Ash Wednesday). I ate breakfast as scheduled at home. Ivan and I drove to the LRCP, and I had blood drawn and took my chemo medications as scheduled.

I waited with Ivan in the main LRCP waiting area on the lower level of Victoria Hospital. About twenty minutes before my radiation appointment, I went into the radiation waiting area and replaced my clothes with a loose one-size-fits-all hospital gown. We had a locker to store our clothes and belongings in, but Ivan always held on to my hospital bag while I was going through radiation. I always smiled to Ivan and waved goodbye before going into the treatment room, as I didn't want him to feel afraid for me.

While waiting for my turn, I usually met other cancer patients. If the patients seemed willing and open, I would talk to them. Some people didn't want to talk, and I respected their silence.

One lady was bitterly heartbroken because her husband had been diagnosed with terminal cancer. A young man had been diagnosed with an orange-size brain tumour; his tumour was a meningioma (on the surface of the brain). He was given strong medication when he was young, and he believed his tumour was a result of the medication. He had two children and fortunately could still work. I also saw a young child (ten years old or maybe younger) waiting for radiation. I felt really sad for her, although I didn't know what her circumstances were. I just imagined how horrible it would be to go through cancer at such a young age. I felt that I somewhat understood the pain of her parents, family and school friends.

On that first day of radiation and chemotherapy, I began two novenas (nine days of special prayers). The first novena was to St. Peregrine (the patron saint of cancer patients) to help me through my treatments. The second novena was to Ste. Thérèse of Lisieux (a well-known young saint who looked at life with love). I prayed for healing, a cure, and courage to undergo the treatments that seemed so foreign and strange to me. I really didn't know exactly what to expect when I started my cancer treatment journey.

After I entered the radiation treatment room, I had to lie flat on my back on a bed. I had to keep my legs straight and propped on a soft moulded cushion. My eye glasses had to be removed so the face mask could be fastened across my head and clicked into place. The secured mask made sure that the radiation treatment was targeted accurately.

Usually two radiation therapists helped to set me up. I needed to be perfectly still while the radiation machine did its "thing." The therapists were very careful to make sure that my alignment was good. They used X-ray beams to ensure alignment accuracy. They also adjusted the height of the flat bed. They then left the room before the radiation started and monitored me through a camera. If I needed any help, I was to raise my hand so they could see it and come in to assist me.

During the radiation, I continuously repeated silently, "Jesus, Our Lady of Guadalupe, have mercy on me. Jesus, Our Lady of Guadalupe, have mercy on me. Jesus, Our Lady of Guadalupe, have mercy on me..."

The radiation usually lasted around twenty-five minutes. When the therapists returned to say, "You're done," I always replied, "Thank God." After releasing me from my face mask, the therapist helped me off the bed with an arm boost.

After my very first session, I broke down and cried. I said that I really needed the radiation to work because I had a one-month-old baby to care for. The therapists were very empathetic and managed to calm me down. I felt so relieved that they understood how desperately I wanted the radiation to work.

I changed back into my regular clothes and saw Ivan again in the waiting area. I updated him on how the radiation went. For example, at some point during the radiation treatment, I heard a "gate" open and saw a flash of bright white light. This happened a few times. It was like a professional photographer was taking my photo and the bright light of the flash came on. I could also hear buzzing sounds from the machine. After the appointment I asked the therapists about the white light, and they said that other patients had talked about it but they didn't know what it was called, and they suggested that I ask the oncologist.

At the start of each week of radiation treatment I had to meet with my radiation oncologist. When my radiation was done, Ivan and I would go to another area to meet with him. We usually met first with a radiation therapist, who would weigh me and ask if I had any concerns or questions for the oncologist.

Ivan and I met with the fellow assigned to my radiation oncologist, the same one who had given us the pathology results, because the oncologist was away that day. As usual, I had my list of questions for her.

I asked her about the white light that I experienced during radiation. She said this phenomena was typical when the brain was radiated, and she would ask my oncologist about it when he returned.

I asked her several questions related to my treatment and learned the following:

- The timing and sequence for taking all my meds were critical for the treatment to be effective.
- I could not miss any medications.
- I needed thirty radiation treatments (with a lower dosage) based on past proven efficacy with other similar cases.
- Since my brain tumour was on my left prefrontal cortex, radiation could possibly impact my eye and brainstem; my dosage was low, and impact would not likely occur.
- It was reasonable to take Advil (a brand of ibuprofen, a nonsteroidal anti-inflammatory drug [NSAID]) for the swollen glands under my chin and ear.

After my appointment, we returned home, and she contacted my neuro-oncologist. My doctor said that I could taper off Dilantin (a phenytoin anti-epileptic drug or anticonvulsant) and start on another anticonvulsant drug (Keppra, generically known as levetiracetam) to control potential seizures by slowing down impulses in my brain.

I continued to take my medications as prescribed for the rest of the first week.

I continued with my radiation and chemotherapy and continued to see the pure white light and hear the sound of a gate or door opening and closing. On the third day, I also noticed a strange smell, like freezer burn, when the light flashed. On the fourth day of radiation (March 17), the white light was brighter and stronger and the odour was still noticeable. The radiation therapists told me that my treatment was the same as usual—nothing new or different.

On the Sunday prior to the second week of chemo and radiation, I had a very stressful day, full of tears caused by an unnecessary family conflict, and my sinuses were congested.

On my second week of radiation and chemotherapy, I saw both my radiation oncologist (with his fellow) and my neuro-oncologist, who prescribed my chemotherapy medications. I learned the following:

- The white light and smell had no name but had been reported previously by others.
- There was no known cause for my brain tumour (it was a rather rare type of malignant brain tumour).
- In the next few weeks, I could expect hair loss, sensitivity on the skin and eyes, and tiredness.
- My progress was tracked by my blood work.
- My loose face mask needed to be reported to the radiation therapists.
- My radiation and chemotherapy oncologists would communicate and coordinate my treatments.
- The vaccinations my baby needed would not impact my chemo or radiation treatments.

On Tuesday, March 22, 2011, we had our six-weeks-after-birth follow-up appointment with our obstetrician. She said that my pathology report was the "most beautiful and well-written report" because of my special circumstance. I believe that by "beautiful" she meant that the surgeons took a lot of care to describe what they saw and did during surgery. She said that I was physically okay, and I would have to ask my oncologists for advice regarding a future pregnancy. We gratefully thanked her again for taking care of Genevieve's birth and being there for us.

At the end of the week, my brother-in-law from Mississauga brought a statue of Our Lady of Guadalupe to our home, and we began a nine-day prayer novena with my parents-in-law. It was March 26, exactly one month after Genevieve's baptism. He also brought a statue of St. Michael the Archangel (patron saint of sickness), an image of Padre Pio of Pietrelcina (a humble Capuchin friar who bore the stigmata [crucifixion wounds] of Christ), and several sets of novena prayers.

When we said our prayers as a family, Genevieve would not make any noise. When it was time to pray she would place both hands together in a prayer position, and when the prayers ended, she would unfold her hands. My parents-in-law witnessed this and called Genevieve our "miracle baby."

On my third week of radiation and chemo, I learned that I could use over-the-counter drugs for my sore throat and sinuses. My blood results showed a low white blood cell count that was consistent with my sinus and throat problems.

Dealing With Hair Loss

After ten days of radiation, my hair began to fall out. My radiation fellow and neuro-oncologist had both warned me about hair loss after ten days. I was surprised they were so precise! Then I thought, "Hey, they should know, because of their experience with other patients."

As I brushed my shoulder-length hair, the hair from the front left of my head fell out with no pain at all. I was sad to see it. Ivan kindly and gently told me, "It's okay. No need to be worried." He said I looked fine with less hair. He didn't want me to feel badly about my hair loss. Ivan "got it" because he was balding himself. He had already lost a majority of his hair due to natural age and stress. It was comforting for me to know that Ivan wasn't worried about my bald spots. I didn't want to look bald and ugly to him.

Since I didn't shave my head, we bought a "hair snare" drain guard from the local hardware store. It was placed over the shower drain and caught hair as I shampooed. It was a round plastic piece with a raised section that was perforated to let water into the drain but keep the hair out. With all the hair I dropped, a cheap little strainer helped to keep the expensive plumbers away.

My hair loss progressively increased. I decided not to shave my head because I thought I could do a "comb-over" to disguise my bald spots. Unfortunately, I had no hairstyling skills to use to disguise my lack of hair. I wore a bandana that I got from the LRCP Cancer Clinic. (See the photos of my hair loss progression in the appendix, figure 1. I did not cut my hair in between the photos taken.)

I started to look like the famous inventor and politician Benjamin Franklin, with a bald top and long hair on the sides. I wore two side po-nytails to minimize finding long hairs on the floor. As I lost more hair, I wore one ponytail at the centre back.

One day while Ivan and I were out shopping, we saw several head-scarves of different colours. We purchased eight beautiful scarves, one for each of the colours of clothing I wore.

19. Treatment Week 4—Giving Thanks and Being Grateful

On my fourth week of radiation and chemotherapy we went to the LRCP as usual. Ivan and I also visited St. Joseph's Hospital with Genevieve. The nurses were happy to see that Genevieve and I were doing well. We met with Shana Da Fonseca, the clever and perceptive nurse who recognized in the emergency room that I had a neurological problem rather than the flu, and gave her a thank-you card. Coincidentally, she is from our church parish and a good friend of one of our neighbours. We realized that God had been helping us all along.

We also met with and thanked the nursing staff who took care of Genevieve when she was at St. Joseph's Hospital and I was still at University Hospital. They were so happy to see Genevieve again. We could see that she felt very comfortable being passed around to the nurses who took care of her when she was born. She didn't cry or fuss with any of them.

The next day, the family home visitor and public health nurse visited us at home to see how Genevieve and I were doing. Genevieve had white pimples on her face, but the nurse said they were normal for a newborn baby.

That evening, Ivan and I attended our first Brain Tumour Support Group meeting. (See part 2 of this book for more details.) We had seen a poster about this meeting at the LRCP, and I was really looking forward to meeting others affected by a brain tumour. Meeting other brain tumour survivors and sharing my story gave me hope to carry on.

20. Treatment Weeks 4, 5 and 6

On April 8, 2011, Ivan and I met with our neuro-oncologist. Often we had to wait a long time to see him. On this particular visit, I was so tired that I had to lie down and use the bed in the exam room to rest until the doctor arrived. I could tell that my energy was quickly depleting. The short nap helped me get through the appointment.

Eventually the oncologist came in. We advised him that our brain surgeon had not yet set up a six-week-after-surgery follow-up appointment. He checked my head scar, which goes from one ear to the other ear (like a hair band), and he noticed that a staple was still in my skull above my ear. On the other side, his nurse noticed a stitch that had not dissolved as it was supposed to. Right there in the examination office, the nurse eagerly removed the staple and the stitch. She was very friendly, and she seemed happy to do some "surgical" work rather than charting or recording.

In my fourth week of treatment, I learned the following from the radiation oncology fellow:

- My blistered or "sunburned" forehead could be calmed with a cool gel, unscented aloe vera lotion or cream.
- She did not recommend that I double up on radiation for the last session.
- There were no concerns with respect to my white blood cell counts.
- It was good news that my menstrual period had resumed because it meant my ovaries were still working. Incidentally, prior to my surgeries and pregnancy my periods were very irregular; brain surgery and pregnancy seemed to have "cured" my irregular periods and stabilized my hormones.

- I could stop taking Tylenol to manage my post-surgeries pain.
- My physical weight was less than my pre-pregnancy weight, and I had maintained the weight through the treatments (+/- 3 pounds).

In my fifth week of treatment, I learned the following from my neuro-oncologist:

- I was progressing as well as other patients had.
- Tiredness would continue.
- Hair loss would continue.
- He also did not recommend that I double up on radiation for my last session because the LRCP clinic was closed on Good Friday.
- We hadn't heard from our University Hospital neurosurgeon for my six-week-post-surgery follow-up; he advised Ivan and me to follow up with the neurosurgeon's secretary. (This we promptly did, but to no avail.)

When we also met with the radiation oncologist's fellow, she advised us of the following:

- We would meet once more after my last radiation treatment; further follow-up would be with my neuro-oncologist.
- More tiredness and hair loss were expected.
- She confirmed that Saturday, April 23, would be my last radiation and chemotherapy treatment for the time being.
- The radiation dosage markers (little round stickers) placed on my forehead the week before showed that the correct amount of radiation had been administered to my brain.
- The metal staple that was found in the side of my skull did not impact my radiation.

In my sixth week of treatment, the radiation oncologist fellow said that my MRI scan was scheduled for May 13, 2011. She also provided us with her pager number in case anything urgent arose. I clearly recall her saying, "You sailed through radiation and chemo." That was very reassuring to hear from the fellow who had first met us with the unsettling news of my pathology results.

My sixth week of treatment was also Holy Week, a very solemn week in the Roman Catholic Church year, leading up to the crucifixion, death and resurrection of Our Lord Jesus Christ.

The LRCP clinic was closed on Good Friday. My chemotherapy and radiation oncologists had agreed that it was not a good option to double up on my radiation on Holy Thursday. I had only one more radiation treatment, on Saturday, April 23. The clinic was only open for special circumstances. I was very fortunate to finish my chemotherapy and radiation treatments before Easter.

On my last day of radiation, I asked the radiation therapists if they keep the masks. They said they have no storage place for them, so they destroy them, but some patients want to personally crush the mask themselves. I asked to keep my mask as a "souvenir" of what I had been through. Unfortunately, because LRCP was closed there was no gong to bang or bell to ring that day. I could not celebrate in style or let others know I was done with treatments.

Nevertheless, God and Our Lady knew, and my family knew too. Alleluia! Alleluia! Thanks be to God! I survived the treatments.

On that last day of my radiation and chemo, Ivan's brother brought his parents back to Mississauga and picked up the statue of Our Lady of Guadalupe and all the accompanying prayers and images.

At the end of April, I told my CCAC physiotherapist and occupational therapists that I was feeling better. No more PT and OT services were needed.

21. MAY 2011—NOVENA TO OUR LADY OF GUADALUPE

TRADITIONALLY IN THE ROMAN CATHOLIC CHURCH, THE MONTHS OF MAY and October are dedicated to Mother Mary, the mother of Jesus Christ.

When my treatments were initially over, I had the month of May as a break. Ivan and I asked our pastor if we could lead a nine-day novena at our church in honour of Our Lady of Guadalupe, who had helped my family through our desperate situation. He didn't hesitate to tell us to go ahead and "trust."

We spoke to the pastor on the Feast of Divine Mercy, one week after Easter Sunday. I believe that the Holy Spirit inspired him to agree to our request. After we got the approval to proceed, we asked Ivan's father if we could borrow his large image of Our Lady of Guadalupe. This framed image is approximately 3 feet wide by 4 feet high. My father-in-law's image was in Mississauga. He also did not hesitate and immediately agreed.

We began to prepare a handout for the nine-day novena. We shared out thoughts with our pastor. Each day we would give some background on Our Lady of Guadalupe and then pray the rosary together. We would conclude the prayers with the memorare prayer to Our Lady. He trusted that we would do well and respectfully honour Her.

In the first week of May 2011, we saw the beatification of Pope John Paul II, prayed on the feast of St. Peregrine, got more information about childcare from our family home visitor, and visited my work colleagues to introduce baby Genevieve to them on my 8th work anniversary. I also celebrated my first Mother's Day; it was all wonderful and special.

Our novena to Our Lady of Guadalupe started on Monday, May 9, 2011, and concluded on Thursday, May 19. My parents-in-law returned by train on the first day of our novena. They looked very tired. We were sure that their time back in their house was exhausting. They had many things to do before resuming care of Genevieve.

My mother-in-law gave Genevieve a small lilac-coloured beaded rosary that she had received from a very nice and religious lady from her parish (St. Joseph) in Mississauga. It fit Genevieve's hand perfectly.

On the first day of the novena, we discussed why we were leading the novena. We explained our experience with Our Lady of Guadalupe and our dedication to her.

A child from the school next door to the church said the rosary prayer very loudly. We later learned that the child had epilepsy and understood my illness (my headaches and seizure). I was amazed that a young child could appreciate and "get it."

On the second day of the novena, Ivan discussed the background history of the time when Our Lady appeared to the native Indians in Mexico. He gave the context for the importance of Our Lady's visit.

Also, our family home visitor came for her regular visit to see how our family was coping with Genevieve's development and my cancer treatments.

On the third day of the novena, Ivan talked about Our Lady's apparitions to native Indian Juan Diego. He explained each of the five apparitions and the message from Our Lady.

The church secretary had put me in contact with Maria Rubio, another parishioner who also had a brain tumour, and we met her on this day. We found out that we had a lot in common—giving birth at an older age than most women, experiencing complications during pregnancy, believing deeply in Our Lady, especially Our Lady of Guadalupe (as Maria's family is from Columbia), and, obviously, having a brain tumour. Fortunately, Maria's tumour was non-cancerous. She had support from her family, who were in London, Ontario, Columbia and Mexico.

On the fourth day of the novena, Ivan presented more details about Juan Diego, as a person, a visionary and an inspired Indian.

We also visited our family doctor for Genevieve's three-month checkup. Genevieve weighed ten pounds, eight ounces. She had gained five pounds six ounces in three months. We were very happy that she had doubled her weight.

On the fifth day of the novena, at 6:30, bright and early in the morning, I had my follow-up MRI scan after the end of radiation and chemotherapy treatments. It was also the feast day of Our Lady of Fatima (who appeared in 1917 in Portugal to three young shepherd children).

In our novena Ivan presented the facts of the basilica in Mexico. The shrine of Our Lady of Guadalupe is accessible by the underground train in Mexico City and is the most visited Roman Catholic shrine after the Vatican.

There was a funeral at our parish, and my piano teacher was playing the music. I knew her from my Mandarin Chinese class, but I did not know that she was a Catholic. She told Ivan that her parents were coming from Saskatchewan to help her with her second pregnancy while her husband was away at a conference.

On the sixth day of the novena, Ivan spoke about the miracle of the tilma, or shawl, that Juan Diego wore when he asked Our Lady for a sign to show the bishop that he had indeed seen and talked to Her. Our Lady wanted a church to be built where She had appeared to Juan Diego and as proof that he had actually seen Her, She left Her image on his tilma and placed non-native flowers on it so that the bishop would believe Juan Diego.

My piano teacher's parents from Saskatchewan attended our novena and even prayed a decade of the rosary with the parishioners. They were strong supporters for our prayers and our goal to find a cure, and we were very touched by their presence and prayers. Their own daughter was experiencing complications with her own pregnancy, and her aunt had a brain tumour, so they truly "got it"; we really appreciated their understanding, compassion and presence at church.

On the seventh day of the novena, Ivan spoke about the features of the tilma. There were several significant characteristics worth noting for those who were interested in Our Lady's magnificent appearance.

On the eighth day of the novena, Ivan presented the symbols in Our Lady's image and the significance of those symbols. He also explained the scientific studies that were done on the tilma to confirm its authenticity.

On the ninth and last day of the novena, I spoke about our search in Mexico for the Chapel of the Fifth Apparition. Ivan's father said that in the book *A Handbook on Guadalupe*,[8] one chapter heading was "When You Go to Guadalupe—Don't Forget Tulpetlac!" We only had a few clues from the book. With the clues written on a little notepad sheet, we asked a taxi driver to help us locate the chapel. After a few twists and turns the driver found it. It was a magnificent visit where we could sense the presence of holiness as soon as we entered the small chapel. We also got to see the well under the altar where Our Lady's water has remained since 1531 when she healed Juan Diego's uncle, who was very sick and near death.

Each day after we said the rosary, several parishioners asked us questions about how to say the novena on their own, shared their own experiences about praying to Our Lady, or wanted to understand more about the significance of the symbols on Juan Diego's tilma. We were happy that our pastor trusted us, and we were pleased to share our love and dedication for Our Lady of Guadalupe with our fellow parishioners at Holy Family Parish.

---

8 The Academy of the Immaculate, *A Handbook On Guadalupe* (Waite Park, MN: Parke Press, 2001), 214.

22. FOLLOW-UP AFTER INITIAL TREATMENTS

THE DAY AFTER WE FINISHED THE NOVENA, IVAN AND I HAD A SCHEDULED follow-up appointment with my oncologists at LRCP. It had already been four weeks since my last radiation and chemotherapy treatments. Time was flying by with all the activities that occupied us.

On Friday, May 20, Ivan and I met with our radiation oncologist's fellow. She told us that there was some swelling evident on my MRI brain scan. No more radiation could be done on my brain, as I had had the maximum dose that a brain can tolerate. She said to expect more tiredness post-radiation and that I would now see my neuro-oncologist for further follow-up treatments. I told her about our planned overseas trip to Asia in August, and she said the trip would be okay. She also said that an eye appointment and dental checkup would be reasonable.

Since I was feeling "normal," she suggested that the MRI scans could be showing swelling rather than regrowth of my tumour. My radiation oncologist joined us and agreed with the fellow and suggested another MRI scan to follow up. He showed us my MRI scans of May 13 and compared them to my post-surgery MRI scan.

There was a noticeable shift of the brain after the surgery to remove the tumour. The centreline, between the left and right hemispheres of the brain, was not straight; it had a noticeable "kink" where the tumour had resided. After the MRI scan taken on May 13, the centreline was clearly straight (vertically, up and down).

The fellow had me do a few typical neurological checks, including the following:

- I walked down the hallway and back again to see if I walked steadily.
- I followed her finger movement with my eyes (up and down, side to side).

- I opened my mouth wide and closed my mouth.
- I squeezed my eyes shut while pretending to hold a pizza with both arms outstretched in front of me.
- I told her where I was.
- I told her the date.
- She checked for asymmetry in my arm and leg reflexes.

There were no signs for concern.

We then met with my neuro-oncologist to get more information about next steps.

My blood tests results were all normal, but he agreed with the fellow that a follow-up MRI scan would still be needed.

The treatment regime going forward would include the following:

- six more months of chemotherapy
- blood tests every three weeks after taking chemo drugs (to check my white blood cell count, which might become low)
- monthly monitoring
- no driving for one month after I stopped taking Dilantin as an anticonvulsant (on May 15, 2011) and started taking another anticonvulsant (Keppra)

The chemotherapy plan going forward would be as follows:

- two hours after eating supper, take antinauseants like Ondansetron (Zofran) for the first five nights (could cause constipation) and then continue with Granisetron (Kytril)
- three hours after eating supper, take chemo medication (Temodal, which can cause severe nausea, taken with water)
- at week 3, give blood samples at LRCP to monitor white blood cell counts; the chemo drug amount would be adjusted accordingly
- repeat for three rounds of chemotherapy
- in early August, get another MRI scan
- have three more months of chemotherapy

At each checkup visit with the oncologist, Ivan helped me to complete a patient survey at a kiosk, using my health card and a personal password. There were several kiosks at the LRCP, and there was usually no waiting involved. The survey asked the cancer patient to report the level he or she was experiencing of the following, on a scale of zero to ten:

- pain
- tiredness
- drowsiness
- nausea
- lack of appetite
- shortness of breath
- depression
- anxiety
- well-being

I also had blood drawn, according to the oncologist's blood requisition form, each time prior to seeing the oncologist. I got to know some of the phlebotomists (technicians who withdraw blood samples) because of my frequency at the blood clinic. I always reminded the attending phlebotomist to count down before putting the needle into my arm and to use a small round bandage on my arm instead of the large three-quarter-inch tape. I always had blood drawn from my right arm because I carried Genevieve in my left arm and tried to avoid stress or bruising in it. I had to drink a lot of water before my blood test so that my veins were more easily located in order for them to insert the needle.

23. JUNE 4, 2011—FIRST SEIZURE

I WOKE UP WITH A TERRIBLE HEADACHE. IVAN TOLD ME TO RELAX. "YOU JUST had a seizure."

I said, "I feel like someone just took a baseball bat to the back of my head." I felt so much pain. He told me to remain flat on my back, and he calmly told me that I had been shaking vigorously for approximately ten minutes and moving erratically in bed. Froth was coming out of my mouth, and he knew I was experiencing a seizure. He let me settle down until I was coherent again.

Ivan called the LRCP and was told to give me three doses of 100 mg of Dilantin at once. He gave me the medication, and I went back to rest.

After the weekend, we followed up with the neuro-oncologist. He said my seizure could have been caused by scar tissue in my brain where the surgery was performed or by growth of the tumour.

He said that I would not be able to drive myself for one whole year after my seizure. I was devastated to hear that news. I recall telling my sister, who is always an optimist. She said, "That's okay." I felt angry and told her, "It's *not* okay!" I would have to depend on someone else, everywhere I wanted to go. I did not like being dependent on Ivan or anyone else. I had always driven myself to work in London and in Toronto (sometimes back and forth in one day). Not being able to drive was a big hit on my sense of independence. It was definitely not okay. She did "not get it." I felt very frustrated.

24. More Appointments

June 20, 2011—Hair Starting to Grow Back

As the oncologists also predicted, my hair started to grow back. My hair came back slightly curly and eventually straightened out. The left front of my head still has no hair and it will likely not re-grow. I recalled the neuro-oncologist reminding me several times that if I had hair like Ivan's, it was not possible that the hair would re-grow.

July 18, 2011—Follow Up With Neuro-oncologist

We met with my neuro-oncologist's substitute, a woman with the same last name as my usual neuro-oncologist. I showed her my head scar, and she suggested monitoring for infections and any redness. She gave me a blood work requisition for before my proposed trip to Asia in August. She was not alarmed or concerned that I was contemplating a long-distance trip.

July 22, 2011—Genevieve's First Words

While Genevieve and I were listening to "Ave Maria" on our CD player, Genevieve said, "Mama." She was so clear. We were so happy to hear her speak. Mostly her "talk" was slobby "blah blah blah." We knew Mother Mary was happy to hear Genevieve say, "Mama."

July 26, 2011—MRI (pre-vacation)

I had my MRI scan done at Victoria Hospital. Nothing extraordinary—same process as usual. (See part 2 of this book for more details about an MRI process.)

Thursday, July 28, 2011—MRI Scan Results

My neuro-oncologist called with the results of my recent MRI scan. He said that there was "something abnormal" on the left side of my brain. It could have been related to treatments, but it was hard to tell from the MRI scan. He gave his honest opinion that he would have concerns with me travelling so far to Asia, where cost and care would be unknown.

Ivan and I felt deeply disappointed. We had already set aside all our things to pack in a separate area of our house. We wanted to alleviate stress by preparing early to go to Asia three days later. It wasn't like we hadn't advised the oncologists of our proposed trip. I collapsed in tears, bearing the sad and unfavourable news. Still in tears, I called those we were going to meet and told them the last-minute news about my MRI results. We reluctantly cancelled our plans to go to Asia.

The neuro-oncologist apologized. He said that he would arrange for a follow-up appointments with my neurosurgeon at University Hospital, to discuss another resection surgery, and with his substitute neuro-oncologist in August.

1st and 2nd Weeks of August 2011—Family and Friends Visit

As usual, we were very busy with visits from family and friends. My eldest sister and her kids, who lived in the United States, drove up to visit us. I don't know how much my nieces and nephews understood about my cancer. They seemed surprised that I had energy and didn't look dead. I often wondered what people expected to see when they visited me. Typically, a visitor would say, "Hey, you look good." That's a very nice compliment, but I wondered if they expected to see me grey, dull, colourless and near-to-death. They never told me. I never dared to ask.

We celebrated Genevieve's sixth month birthday and bought her a high chair. Genevieve loved eating solid foods instead of mush. She enjoyed eating at her high chair and would say, "Muh, muh" for "More, more."

We had a visit from my former boss from 1998. He always brought lots of cheer and good wishes from his family. His wife had survived cancer many years earlier. They had also gone to Mexico, and shortly thereafter they conceived their only daughter. His wife understood and "got it" about being an "older" mom with cancer and a baby.

Genevieve's godfather also visited and brought beautiful fresh flowers to brighten our day. His wife was Ivan's and my theology teacher in high school. Unfortunately, his wife did not win her battle with breast cancer in 2005. She was a wonderful and caring individual, with lots of positive energy. Genevieve's godfather really "got it" and always asked sincerely how I was doing. Having three little girls when his wife was sick was an arduous journey. Ivan and I had helped where we could. We unfortunately did not then appreciate how cancer can totally change your life. My teacher had also had a large family. She unfortunately did not receive the family support she expected, although she was like a mother to her younger siblings. Her husband understood and "got it" when I said that only a few from my large family were understanding or supportive.

We now understood and appreciated his concern for us. He, of everyone we knew well, could comprehend our circumstances and our need for help and support. He understood that it was hard for Ivan and me to be humble and ask for help.

A work colleague of mine also visited us and played with Genevieve. She said that many people sent their good wishes to me. She also told me that many people missed me, and what I brought to the team (the courage to speak up) was greatly lacking. That was very nice to hear because I knew I had worked hard at my job and was dedicated to my team, colleagues and other staff.

August 15, 2011—Follow-Up with Neuro-oncologist

After the visiting and good fun, on Monday, August 15, we met with my neuro-oncologist's substitute. We had forms from the Canada Pension Plan (CPP) and my health care insurance provider that had to be completed by our neuro-oncologist. The neuro-oncologist's nurse said that she would have my actual oncologist complete the forms when he returned.

The substitute came into the exam room to say again that my tumour seemed to be growing or was possibly in "pseudo-progression" (it appeared like it was growing but actually was not). She offered us three options to consider:

- Continue with daily Temodal at a lower dosage; check blood every two weeks instead of three weeks. The brain tumours of about 23 percent of the patients who chose this option did not grow within the following six months.
- Try another chemotherapy drug, lomustine, one day for six weeks; it would be harsher on the blood cells and worse for myelosuppression (a decrease in blood cell production) and harder on the overall body. The brain tumours of 19 percent of the patients who chose this option did not grow, and there was less shrinkage of the brain tumour.)
- Try another chemotherapy drug, bevacizumab (or Avastin), which had been used for treating colon cancer and was provided through intravenous means. The drug would be injected every two weeks. Avastin was a relatively new medication and was not covered by most drug plans. It was used more commonly in the United States than in Canada. The downside was the cost, which was very high. For example, a seventy kilogram person would incur a $1,500 charge for each treatment. Forty percent of patients who chose this option saw no further tumour growth and saw tumour shrinkage.

We told the substitute that we would choose the first option, since the other options could be viable later on if necessary.

If I had any symptoms like weakness in my body, slurred speech, bad headaches, and so on, I would be given steroids (like dexamethazone), but I needed to let the LRCP know.

The neuro-oncologist's substitute gave me prescriptions for the steroid dexamethazone and Septra, an antibiotic, to be taken with Temodal. I would need to take one tablet three times a week. She took my blood pressure which was low, 90/60, where "normal" is usually 120/80.

The substitute showed Ivan and me my MRI scans from February 10 and compared it with the recent scan from July 26. The actual left side of the brain appears as the right side of the brain on the MRI image, and conversely, the actual right side appears as the left side of the brain. The images from scans taken at different times can be compared side by side digitally to note any changes in tumour size and location. The brain tumour still appeared large on the recent scan, even after surgery, radiation, chemotherapy, and three further rounds of chemo. There was a distinct shift in the centre line between the two brain hemispheres.

August 18, 2011—Visit to Precious Blood Sisters

Our pastor coordinated a visit with the Precious Blood Sisters in a convent in London. He had asked them to pray for our family and then asked us if we wanted to meet them. Although I went to mass at Brescia College while I attended the University of Western Ontario, I never knew that there was a convent behind Brescia College. Our pastor was on vacation, but he agreed to introduce us to the Sisters of the Precious Blood. My in-laws were with us.

Our pastor also wanted us to see the image of Our Lady of Guadalupe in the convent. He asked me to tell them about my brain cancer journey and having a baby on the same day as my surgery. The sisters were happy to meet the family they were all praying for. It was wonderful to put a face to a name. We felt very honoured that the pious sisters were praying for our family.

Genevieve was very comfortable being passed from one sister to another. She remained calm and did not make any noise. She was awake and saw gentle loving smiles.

August 19, 2011—Local Apothecary Visit

A credible source advised me that soursop—also known as graviola, *guanabana* in Spanish, and *corossol* in French—was a good anti-cancer fruit. Friends told us that we could buy the juice at our local grocery store.

They also confirmed that when they were kids, their South American or Central American parents would tell them to eat guanabana because it was good for overall health.

We met with a local apothecary in London, Ontario, who helped us do some research on the benefits of taking soursop. The apothecary said that he could not find any scientific proof that soursop could cure cancer. It was a legend of elders that soursop was a powerful healing fruit. The apothecary said he had researched the tropical plant database and found no results to show the benefits of soursop's fruit, leaves, stems or bark.

August 23, 2011—Novena Prayers at Maria's House

We were invited to go to Maria Rubio's house for a novena. Maria was in need of prayers also. She had a benign brain tumour. A Polish couple in London was bringing images of Our Lady of Guadalupe, Jesus Divine Mercy and St. Padre Pio and prayer booklets for families to pray for nine consecutive days. I joined Maria's family on this particular evening. I saw that the whole setup, with flowers and candles, was similar to the statues that my brother-in-law had brought to us from Mississauga. We prayed the rosary and Divine Mercy Chaplet, sang songs and added our petitions. We prayed together for about one hour. It was a very special and prayerful evening.

August 24, 2011—Participating in the "Look Good Feel Better" Program

I invited Maria to join me for a cancer patients' Look Good Feel Better program, where women from the cosmetics industry show cancer patients how to feel better using makeup products. This session was provided for women going through cancer treatments and those who had already completed treatment and wanted to look better. I rarely wear makeup, but I thought that it would be something nice to do with Maria.

Ivan drove both of us to the LRCP. We joined other women with cancer and enjoyed using different makeup products.

The organizers gave each cancer patient a box of makeup: facial creams, eyeliners, lipsticks, makeup remover, eye shadow, and more. We got to use the makeup and try different styles. At the end of the session, the organizers gave each of us a long-stem red rose, and we got to keep the box of products that we used.

We also learned about different kinds of wigs, natural versus synthetic. It was all very interesting and worthwhile to attend. Maria and I enjoyed the session, and she got to take home a rose too.

August 29, 2011—Basement Water Leak

Ivan and I were preoccupied with getting Genevieve adjusted to daycare, getting through my cancer treatments, and finding a good nanny. Then heavy rains came, and water started pouring into our basement. We thought that we had sourced the leak, and we hired a contractor to dig up our window well and seal the crack from the outside. It worked for a short time, but the water still came back inside.

August 29 (Same Day)—Meeting with Neurosurgeon— Another Surgery?

My neuro-oncologist had set up an appointment for me with my neurosurgeon at University Hospital. The neurosurgeon said that if my neuro-oncologist recommended surgery, he could do another resection of my brain. I felt like I was in a circular conversation where my oncologist referred me to my neurosurgeon, who then referred me back to my original oncologist.

The neurosurgeon said the growth of my brain tumour was in a "relatively quiet area" of my brain, and chemotherapy could be more effective after another surgery to remove more tumour. We would need to consider when would be a good time to perform the surgery. We'd have to think about recovery time also, in the hospital and at home.

The risks associated with surgery included the following:

- multiple surgeries thereafter and scar tissue not healing well
- paralysis due to the tumour being so close to critical veins in my brain
- hemorrhaging (profuse bleeding) in the brain

Before my initial surgery in February, my tumour was very compressed, like a sponge. Now my tumour was smaller, and it would be easier to remove more effectively. This was an advantage to consider.

The neurosurgeon showed us the four MRI scans taken thus far— pre-surgery (February 8), post-surgery, on May 13 and on July 26. The pre-surgery scan showed a large tumour mass—almost looking like a full moon. The more recent scan (July 26) showed the tumour like a fetus shape.

After talking to the neurosurgeon, Ivan and I thought that the risks of another surgery would be more problematic than to continue with the current chemotherapy regime.

September 4, 2011—Genevieve's First Haircut

At seven months, Genevieve had enough hair to cut. Her spikey crown was getting taller and longer. We took her to Melonheads, a store specializing in children's haircuts, in Mississauga. She sat in a bright orange airplane with a steering wheel while her hair was being cut. She looked so cute and so much neater after her haircut.

September 12, 2011—Follow-Up with Neuro-oncologist

Ivan and I discussed our meeting with the neurosurgeon with our neuro-oncologist. We decided to wait until the next MRI scan in October to see whether to proceed with surgery.

We talked to the neuro-oncologist about graviola (soursop). He said that it was an herbal product that had not been tested as a medicine.

We also spoke to him about an American doctor, Dr. Burzynski, who advocated antineoplastons. He strongly advised against Dr.

Burzynski's treatment. There were no scientifically valid reports to support his claims, especially those about healing childhood cancers.

We informed our neuro-oncologist that my long-term disability benefit was approved by my company's health care insurance provider.

We also told him that we were considering hiring a nanny to help with childcare and housework. We asked him to write a letter that we could send to Canada Revenue Agency (CRA) to support the Labour Market Opinion (LMO) review. He said that he would help us. He would write the letter and send it to us at home. (Refer to part 2 of this book for more information about hiring a nanny.)

I told the neuro-oncologist that I was participating in the LRCP's Soul Medicine program, and he had no objection or comment. (Part 2 of this book provides further details and the insights I gained from this valuable program.)

We reviewed the medications I was taking. The neuro-oncologist told us that my blood test results were fine. I could go to the dentist for general dental cleaning and would not need to take an antibiotic beforehand.

After the previous appointment I had a cold. An over-the-counter decongestant and Tylenol for aches and pains were suitable. I also had headaches, due to stress or high temperature and humidity, and took Extra Strength Tylenol. He said that Tylenol was acceptable.

Mid-September to Early October 2011—Major House Repairs

Literally, when it rains, it pours. We had lots of rain, and it started coming through our chandelier in our hallway. It was like we had a two-storey shower head in our main corridor. Needless to say, it was time to replace our roof. Our house was thirteen years old. I believe that it was a model home for two years before the builder put it up for sale in 2000. Most homes in our neighbourhood were already replacing their roofs. We didn't have much of a choice once the rains came.

In early October, we bit the bullet and asked a contractor to do some "crack stitching" in our basement foundation wall to prevent water from entering. It was a costly exercise, in addition to having to replace the roof.

October 8, 2011—Begin Novena Prayers

Maria Rubio from our parish told us how to get the images of Our Lady of Guadalupe, Jesus (Our Divine Mercy), and Padre Pio and associated prayers. A Polish couple in London was bringing these images around to various homes. I contacted the couple, and the wife asked us to clear a section of one room in our house. They brought the images and prayer booklets to our house. The wife meticulously set everything up on easels and placed flowers around them. She also brought a large candle to make the environment more prayerful. The couple showed us how to say the prayers in the booklet. The wife was very particular and explicit about how the prayers were said and how the images and flowers were set up.

She explained that she and her husband were sharing the images of Our Lady of Guadalupe, Divine Mercy Jesus, and Padre Pio and prayers on behalf of a lady in Mississauga named Dory Tan who saw Our Mother Mary in 1996, near Marmora, Ontario.

My parents-in-law returned to London after the start of our novena. We explained that these images were from Dory Tan in Mississauga. My in-laws then immediately said that they knew of a "Dory" in their parish church. At that moment, we made the startling connection that Dory Tan was from my in-law's parish, St. Joseph in Mississauga.

Before that, they did not know that Dory had visions from Our Lady. They said Dory was a humble and quiet person. She was always deep in prayer before and after mass at church. It was actually Dory who had given Ivan's mom the lilac-coloured rosary. She had given that very same rosary to Genevieve earlier in May, when we did our novena to Our Lady of Guadalupe in our parish. I recalled that my mother-in-law had said this lady was a very pious person and often generously gave lots of religious items to them. It was such a divine and remarkable moment when we made the connection to Dory Tan, a faithful servant to Our Lady and Jesus, Our Merciful Redeemer.

My father-in-law also has deep devotion to Padre Pio. We were happy to say prayers to St. Pio for our intentions. We thought again, we don't meet people in our lives "by accident." Everything that happens in our lives, happens for a reason, if we are following God's plan and will.

October 11, 2011 - Follow-Up with Neuro-oncologist

We thanked our neuro-oncologist for the Labour Market Opinion letter. We still needed his assessment for my long-term care insurance provider.

I typically did not take the flu vaccination. He recommended that I take the it and to ask those close to me to take the flu shot also.

He recommended that I not take the anti-nausea drug (Perchlorperazine), to prevent long-term side effects of tremors. I stopped taking the anti-nausea drug on October 16, 2011, and there were no resultant problems.

October 15, 2011—Brain Tumour Info Day

I spoke to a work colleague whose young daughter had a brain tumour, and he recommended the Brain Tumour Info Day held annually in London as a good place to learn from experts more about tumours and how others are managing. Brain Tumour Info Days were located in several provinces across Canada and were hosted by the Brain Tumour Foundation of Canada.

We attended the Info Day at the Sheraton Hotel in London. We found the seminars interesting. I met a lady whose husband had just recently passed away from the same tumour that I had, GBM IV. She seemed very curious to know more about the disease because she wanted to understand more about how it caused her husband's death.

We saw others from the Brain Tumour Support Group and got caught up with how everyone was doing.

Sunday, October 16, 2011—End of Novena and Prioritizing Our Lives

We ended our nine-day novena to Our Lady of Guadalupe, Jesus and Padre Pio on this day. The Polish couple came to our house to pick up the images. Maria Rubio and her daughter joined us also. We said the prayers together, and at the end of our prayers, our candles went out on their own. The Polish man noticed the candles right away. We spent some time talking about how my parents-in-law knew Dory Tan because she attended the same parish they did in Mississauga. They were amazed that we made the connection. Indeed, what a small world! God puts us all in the right place at the right time. This incident made me think of a verse in the book of Ecclesiastes: "There is an appointed time for everything, and a time for every affair under the heavens" (Ecclesiastes 3:1). I firmly believe that God is a great genius who puts his sons and daughters together when problems seem insurmountable. God does not leave us alone. He is always with us. Often God reminds us in the Bible, "Do not be afraid" (as stated in John 6:20).

We finished our novena but unfortunately had to miss the baptism of Ivan's niece, his brother's only daughter. We also missed the second birthday of Ivan's nephew, his other brother's son, in Mississauga. It was not an easy choice to make, but we knew the novena had to be our priority over other family functions. We realized that we'd gone back to Mississauga for so many celebrations that now we had to prioritize our own family activities, and we started to make decisions based on our priorities rather than those of others. This may sound selfish, but we realized that we were living to other's expectations. We were burning ourselves out in the process. We wanted to please others and not disappoint them. We finally realized that it was not worth compromising our own health and well-being to make everyone else happy; we just simply couldn't please everyone anymore. It was a difficult decision to make, and eventually others who "got it" began to understand that we had different family priorities to consider now.

October 25, 2011—MRI Scan

I had another MRI scan as usual.

October 31, 2011—Meeting with LRCP Social Worker

Ivan and I met with the LRCP social worker to follow up about Merrymount and how I was coping. The social worker advised that my neuro-oncologist would need to write a letter to support my change from short-term disability to long-term disability.

The social worker also recommended that I check the *Mummy Diaries* videos at Wellspring, a centre for cancer patients and their caregivers. The videos discuss situations where moms with incurable diseases communicated with their children about their diseases.

October 31, 2011 - Follow-Up with Neuro-oncologist

The neuro-oncologist's substitute met us to review my MRI scans of October 25, 2011. The scans showed no further tumour growth, and that was great news. As usual, she did the typical neurological tests to assess me. I continued with the Temodal, and my blood work was still fine. My blood pressure seemed low (100/70). The neuro-oncologist said that he would monitor the enhancement near my right optical nerve. "Enhancement" was a location where there was excessive blood flow.

November 7, 2011—Chest Pains

I visited my colleagues in our Toronto office and brought Genevieve with me. After lunch, I felt a strong pressing pain on my chest. I rested for a half hour, and the pain subsided. The next day, we took Genevieve to Merrymount. I continued to feel a strong pressing pain in my chest. I took deep breaths in and out, and the pain slowly subsided once again. We also prayed for the pain to go away, and it did.

November 17, 2011—Family Doctor Visit, Then Chest Pains Continue

I had my physical done with my family doctor. I had blood drawn and updated the doctor on my MRI and results. She did the typical tests: weight, blood pressure (110/70), breast lump test, and pap smear. Nothing new was detected, so I left the office feeling well.

In the evening, while trying to feed Genevieve, I continued to feel a strong pressing pain in my chest. I could feel the pain radiating through my shoulders and back. I told Ivan, "I cannot breathe very well. I feel like something heavy is pressing on my chest." I tried to push on my solar plexus, but pushing aggravated the pain more. I needed Ivan to help me finish feeding Genevieve. I could not even rest on my back, because the pain felt worse. We both prayed to Our Lady of Guadalupe to help control the pain. The pain slowly dissipated. After my stomach made some gurgling sounds, I finally felt relief. I prayed that the pains were nothing more than indigestion.

November 22, 2011—Chest Pains Resume Again

I felt chest pains early in the morning (around 2:30). The pain centred at my diaphragm and radiated out to my back. It felt more painful when I was on my back than when sitting upright. I took Extra Strength Tylenol (500 mg) around 7:25 a.m., but the pains continued. Ivan called the LRCP triage nurse, who recommended that we go to the hospital emergency room.

We took Genevieve to Merrymount and advised the staff that we might not be able to pick her up on time, given the uncertainty of wait times at the hospital. Ivan immediately took me to University Hospital because he believed that the cardiac care at UH would be good. We got through triage and registration and then to the acute care room, where a nurse and then a doctor came to see me. My blood pressure, temperature and heart rate were measured, and all were normal. An ECG (electrocardiogram, which monitors the electrical activity of the heart) performed at 10:30 a.m. showed nothing of concern. Bloodwork was done right after the ECG.

The ER doctor suggested two possibilities for the pain. Since I was on chemotherapy treatment, he said,

- There could be a buildup of fluid around my heart due to some chemotherapy drugs. He recommended that an ultrasound be done on my heart.
- There could be a problem with my lungs. He recommended an X-ray of the lungs.

He also recommended that I take morphine to calm the pain, but I refused the morphine.

A portable ultrasound machine was brought to my bed to check my heart. All appeared fine—no fluid buildup.

When I needed to urinate, the medical team asked for a sample.

At noon, after the urine sample was given, I took two Tylenol 3 (with 325 mg of acetaminophen and 30 mg of codeine). My blood pressure and vitals (temperature and heart rate) were taken again, and there were no concerns.

At 12:25 p.m. I was given saline on a slow drip through an intravenous line. After five minutes, I was taken for my chest X-ray.

At 2:05 p.m., my blood pressure and vitals were again measured. Once again, there were no concerns.

At 5:50 p.m. the ER doctor returned and said that the results of my scans were still not available. I needed to take my anticonvulsant medications and eat something. I did not want to be late to take my chemotherapy medicines. I managed to have a sandwich and water.

At 6:30 p.m. my ER doctor said his shift was ending and another doctor would take over my case. The new doctor said that he would wait until 7:00 p.m. for my scan results.

At 7:05 p.m., I had my anticonvulsant medication with apple juice and water. At 7:15 p.m., there were still no results posted online from my scans. The doctor said the radiologist was coming back to the hospital to dictate my report.

The ER doctor pressed on my stomach and said that I might have a gall bladder problem. He recommended that I have an ultrasound on my stomach just to be sure. In the meantime, he suggested that I have Toradol intravenously, to control the pain. Toradol is an anti-inflammatory and mild blood thinner. He checked for any drug interactions with my chemotherapy drug.

At 7:30 p.m. he returned and advised that there were no interactions and provided me with six Tylenol 3 tablets to take as needed to control the pain. He recommended that I take no more than two Tylenol 3 tablets every four hours, and he cautioned that Tylenol 3 might cause mild nausea and constipation.

At 7:40 p.m., the doctor returned and said that there were no concerns with my scans. He ordered a liver function test to be done from my blood samples. The results would be known the next day.

At 7:45 p.m. the nurse returned to administer Toradol and give me the Tylenol 3 tablets. She told me that my ultrasound was scheduled for 9:30 a.m. the next day. I would need to wait about three hours after the ultrasound to get the results. I had to be back at the emergency department at least thirty minutes before the ultrasound and could not eat after midnight. I was finally discharged from the ER at 8:15 p.m.

There Are No Coincidences in Life

As soon as I was discharged, Ivan and I drove straight to Merrymount to pick up Genevieve. It was about 8:30 p.m. when we stood in front of Merrymount's front door. Everything seemed closed, and not many lights were on in the centre. As we were knocking on the door, a car pulled up to the entrance. Out of the car came out my hairdresser. My hairdresser?

I wondered what she was doing here too so late at night. She told us that her daughter attended sessions at Merrymount; she hadn't known that my daughter was also there. She said that she always rang the doorbell at nighttime. Ivan and I didn't even know to look for a doorbell. We were relieved that she had shown up in our time of need.

Our panic was further eased when we found out that the caregiver was someone that Genevieve liked. We were both very happy and grateful that my chest pain had subsided, my hairdresser surprisingly came to our aid, and Genevieve had a familiar and good caregiver to watch her at Merrymount.

"God doesn't give us more than we can handle." We started the day with great worry and anxiety on our minds but ended the day with joy and gratitude in our hearts.

November 23, 2011—Ultrasound Scans

The next morning, we dropped Genevieve off at Merrymount at 8:25 and then headed back to University Hospital. My abdomen ultrasound and leg Doppler started at 9:30 a.m. as scheduled. The scans took about one hour. I could then eat and have my anticonvulsant tablets.

At 11:50 a.m. the nurse practitioner said that my ultrasound showed no chance of pulmonary embolism. There were a few stones in my gall bladder, which was common after a recent pregnancy and for my age.

The gall bladder stones probably caused all my pain the day before. The stones can cause blockage and inflammation, and infection could result. Fatty foods can cause the gall bladder to produce a bile salt, which is deposited in the liver to help absorb some of the fat in the body. The salt was a precursor to a stone forming. The nurse practitioner said that the stone had probably passed, since my irritation was milder the next day. He consulted with the ER doctor and recommended my discharge.

I was discharged at 12:15 p.m., relieved that after all the tests my pains were controllable by minimizing my intake of greasy foods.

November 25 and 26, 2011—Chest Pains Continue

I continued to take ibuprofen to manage inflammation in my chest and pain from the gall bladder stones.

November 27, 2011—Headache

I experienced pain around the back of my head. My nap was longer than usual (about 4.5 hours), and I slept early in the evening too.

November 28, 2011—Visit with the Neuro-oncologist

We updated my chemotherapy nurse and neuro-oncologist about my gall bladder stones and the visit to University Hospital's ER, including the medications I had and the tests that were done.

We asked the neuro-oncologist about a new glioblastoma multiforme drug called Gliadel, by Eisai Limited. He said it was not a new drug. It had been around for about ten years, but a new company had taken it over. It was a Carmustine implant, a dime-sized wafer used more in the United States than in Canada, and was "not terribly effective." This drug can cause infection and made it harder for scar tissue to heal. Subsequent MRI scans would be hard to interpret.

My follow-up included blood work to be done in two weeks, on December 12, 2011. The oncologist noted that my next appointment with him would be December 23, 2011. Another MRI scan was booked for January 30, 2012.

November 29, 2011—Headache and Body Aches

In the morning I had another headache at the top centre of my head and felt pressure pains at my temples. I took one Extra Strength Tylenol. I began to shiver in the afternoon and bundled myself up in multiple blankets. I took another Tylenol to deal with my fever and headache. I took it again in the evening. My body felt achy and sore. It hurt to move or walk. It felt better to be flat and still in bed. I think the pain may have been because it was raining heavily outside.

November 30, 2011—Weakness Continues

In the morning, I tried to prepare Genevieve's cereal for breakfast, but I couldn't measure any weight for her cereal. I felt frustrated and worn out. Ivan had to take over for me. I went back to bed and slept some more. I woke up again and had a little food and went to bed again. Though my body was still achy and stiff, I managed to go with Ivan to pick up Genevieve from Merrymount at the end of the day.

December 1, 2011—Still Aching

The next day, my body still felt achy. My phlegm was greenish-yellow. This pain was ongoing for about a week. Could this pain be from a strep throat infection?

December 19 to 21, 2011—Stomach Flu

I believe I caught the stomach flu from my daughter, who was at daycare and mixing with other children. I vomited and had diarrhea for at least three days. Genevieve recovered well because her body was relatively small. Ivan was hit really hard, worse than me. We joked that my chemo drugs kept the flu virus under control. The flu really weakened all of us, but somehow we managed to pull through.

December 23, 2011—Meeting with Neuro-oncologist

Ivan, Genevieve and I met with my neuro-oncologist and explained that we were over the stomach flu. He suggested that his substitute give me a Montreal Cognitive Assessment (MoCA) test. I learned from a website that the test "was designed as a rapid screening instrument for mild cognitive dysfunction. It assesses different cognitive domains: attention and concentration, executive functions, memory, language, visuoconstructional skills, conceptual thinking, calculations, and orientation."[9] She administered the test, and she said that I did well.

I gave my neuro-oncologist the long-term disability forms from my health insurance provider for him to complete and return to us. I mentioned that he had one month to complete the forms.

Genevieve was with us for this December appointment. She had been reluctant to take a picture with Santa at the local mall. When we were at the LRCP, there was a small Santa that was the same size as Genevieve. She stood beside him, and we got a photo of Genevieve with a little Santa.

January 2, 2012—A New Year—Headache on Left Side of Head

We went to our niece's birthday party, and there was soft music playing. After the event, I had a terrible headache on the left side of my head. I took two ibuprofen tablets in the evening to allay the pain.

---

9 "Montreal Cognitive Assessment," Cognitive Atlas, http://cognitiveatlas.org/task/Montreal_Cognitive_Assessment.

January 12, 2012—Headache All Around Head

I woke up with a bad headache all around my head. It was raining that day. Sometimes, I got headaches when the exterior pressure changed.

January 30, 2012—MRI Scan

The contrast dye needle was put into my right arm as usual. Moving my right arm was excruciatingly painful. After a little while, the numbness went away. At least the pain did not last for the whole day.

January 31, 2012—Feeling Numb Again

I felt very tired because of my period and loss of blood. I also felt numbness in my right arm where the MRI contrast dye was injected the day before. My right arm was difficult to move and I used my left arm to get the blood to circulate. The numbness eventually disappeared by the evening.

February 3, 2012 - Queasy

I got up feeling very queasy in the morning. I did not take any over-the-counter medication.

Saturday, February 4, 2012—Flu Again?

I had a runny nose and felt very congested. I had diarrhea in the afternoon after my nap. I stayed in bed practically the whole day. I had to calm my stomach with a hot beanbag. I ate very plain food—nothing greasy or spicy.

Monday, February 6, 2012—Follow-Up With Neuro-oncologist—Tumour Spread

I updated my neuro-oncologist's nurse about my headaches, stiff right arm after MRI contrast dye and my "flu" symptoms.

There were no residents to assess me before the neuro-oncologist saw me. He said that the MRI scans of January 30 showed good news and bad news. The good news was that the scan showed a reduction in the size of my brain tumour on the left hemisphere. Unfortunately, the bad news was a new growth showed up on the right hemisphere near the spinal fluid cavity. The neuro-oncologist speculated that the tumour cells could have migrated along the corpus callosum (a structure in the brain that links the left and right hemispheres and helps the two hemispheres communicate). Neuroanatomist Jill Bolte Taylor called the corpus callosum "the highway for information transfer" when she described the brain in layperson's terms in order to explain her stroke and healing process.[10]

The cause of the spread of the tumour was unknown. The location of the tumour near the spinal fluid cavity would be difficult to operate on and navigate. Radiation was not an option as I had had the maximum amount of radiation that a brain could have.

The neuro-oncologist concluded that the Temodal drug was no longer effective in controlling my brain tumour's growth. He suggested another drug called CeeNU (or lomustine), which had been used to treat lung cancer and kidney cancer and could also penetrate the blood-brain barrier like Temodal.

The neuro-oncologist explained the side effects of lomustine:

- It lowered white blood cell counts, so I would be more prone to infections; my blood would need to be closely and regularly monitored.
- It could cause problems with my lungs, but they would occur later on, especially in people with weak lungs.
- It could cause nausea, so an anti-nausea medication would be prescribed to counter this side effect.

The treatment regime for lomustine was for the drug to be taken orally, about once every six to seven weeks. My blood would be monitored regularly to check my immune system. Temodal treatment would

10 Jill Bolte Taylor, *My Stroke of Insight* (New York: Penguin Random House, 2008), 15.

stop immediately that day. I needed to give my body time to "heal" from taking Temodal. A blood test would be done on February 21, 2012 (after the Family Day holiday). The neuro-oncologist would review the blood test results that day and advise me if I could proceed with the anti-nausea medication and lomustine.

The period between doses of lomustine would vary according to the blood test results. Lomustine was not usually used more than six to eight times, because of its harsh side effects.

The neuro-oncologist suggested that I have another MRI scan within three months' time. In that period, I would have taken lomustine twice, and we could then determine if it was effective in shrinking the new tumour in the right brain hemisphere.

The neuro-oncologist also talked to me about a return to work date. He said that given the recent spread of my tumour, he could not recommend that I return to work.

February 21, 2012—Follow-Up with Neuro-oncologist

As scheduled and per the blood requisition, I went to LRCP after two weeks and had blood drawn. I saw the neuro-oncologist's nurse. She told me that the neuro-oncologist said that I could begin the lomustine treatment that night.

Ivan and I were concerned about Genevieve needing to have her scheduled vaccinations at 12 months and 15 months. She now needed her varicella vaccine. The LRCP pharmacist and neuro-oncologist's nurse both agreed that the vaccine was not "live" so I should not be concerned with interference with my lomustine use.

That evening, I began my lomustine treatment. One hour before taking lomustine, I took two 1 mg tablets of Granisetron Hydrochloride for anti-nausea. The lomustine consisted of three tablets (1 of 100 mg and 2 of 40 mg). I had explained to the LRCP pharmacist that I found it difficult to swallow large tablets. She "got it" and gave me smaller tablets. I took all the chemo medication with water. I found it difficult to swallow the second (40 mg) lomustine tablet. I started to throw up and sat in a corner to support my back and heaved into a bucket. I felt awful and went to sleep.

April 2, 2012—Follow-Up with Neuro-oncologist

I had blood drawn as per the neuro-oncologist's requisition. A first year resident evaluated me and did the typical neurological tests like checking my reflexes, walking down the hallway, etc. The neuro-oncologist's nurse advised me that my hemoglobin and platelets were low from the previous week. The blood tests were done on March 12 (three weeks after initial lomustine start).

My neuro-oncologist advised me that my white blood cells were low this time, so I could not start the second round of the lomustine treatment. He suggested that I wait another week and do another blood test. The blood test results would determine if I could continue with lomustine. He said that the next dosage would be lower, to avoid any adverse problems with the white blood cell counts.

I showed my neuro-oncologist both my thumbnails, which appeared bruised near the nail bed (or "lunula"/half-moon). He suspected that the cause was related to my low hemoglobin and platelets.

He reaffirmed that Genevieve could continue with her required vaccinations and that they would not interfere with my treatments.

April 10, 2012—More Blood Tests

I had blood drawn at the LRCP blood lab in the morning. That afternoon, the neuro-oncologist's nurse called to say that my white blood cell counts were still too low (1.2); I needed to have a white blood cell count of at least 1.5 to be able to start my second round of lomustine. She said my platelets were fine at 2.8 and that the neuro-oncologist suggested that I wait another week before taking lomustine.

Sunday, April 15, 2012—Headache Again

I had another headache and took one Extra Strength Tylenol in the evening, to manage the pain.

Monday, April 16, 2012—Headache Continued

In the morning, I had blood drawn at the LRCP blood lab.

My headache continued, and I took an Extra Strength Tylenol tablet in the afternoon. There were many tornadoes in the mid-west United States, so perhaps the environmental pressure change caused my headaches. I was not 100 percent certain, but I found that I was often susceptible to environmental pressure changes that I could feel in my head.

That afternoon, my neuro-oncologist's nurse called to advise that my leukocyte count was 0.5 and my white blood cell count was 3.2. She relayed the neuro-oncologist's message that I could take lomustine that evening. This would be the second time for taking lomustine.

Ivan always helped me to take my chemotherapy medications. We started the chemotherapy as follows:

- two (1 mg) Granisetron for anti-nausea
- one hour later, two tablets of lomustine (100 mg and 40 mg, or 140 mg in total)

Tuesday, April 17, 2012—No Anti-nausea

In the morning, I did not take any anti-nausea tablets after my chemotherapy.

Wednesday, April 18, 2012—Queasy

I felt queasy in the afternoon after my rest. The queasiness returned in the evening too. Thankfully, I did not vomit at all.

May 7, 14, and 22, 2012—More Blood Tests

I had blood drawn again at the LRCP blood clinic per my neuro-oncologist's three requisitions.

May 23, 2012—MRI Scan

I had my usual MRI scan. A line was inserted in my right arm in readiness for my contrast dye to be given during my scan.

This time, there was a Sesame Street Elmo sticker inside the MRI chamber. Genevieve simply adored Elmo. She carried an Elmo stuffed toy every day to her daycare. I felt comforted that "Genevieve" was with me in the MRI machine.

May 24, 2012—Numbness

In the early morning, around 3 a.m., I felt numbness in my right arm. It lasted for at least a half hour. Again, I believed the pain was from my MRI contrast needle.

May 28, 2012—Follow-Up With Neuro-oncologist (Tumour Growth)

The MRI scan of May 23 showed more growth of the tumour on the right hemisphere. The left hemisphere showed no further tumour growth. The neuro-oncologist showed us the MRI scans of January 30 and compared them to the one from May 23.

Since the chemotherapy drug lomustine did not shrink the tumour, we needed to consider some other chemotherapy options, like Etoposide and Avastin.

Etoposide is a chemotherapy drug taken orally every day for twenty-one days, followed by one to two weeks off. The drug was used to treat lung cancer, ovarian cancer, some leukemias and lymphomas, and recurring brain tumours. The adverse side effects of Etoposide include nausea, and it affects the blood cells. If Etoposide was administered intravenously, another side effect would be more hair loss, and it would be less effective for treating brain cancer.

The neuro-oncologist told us that Etoposide wasn't necessarily the best option at that point in time. Etoposide might have helped, but he did not recommend it. The alternative was Avastin.

Avastin was a chemotherapy that was administered intravenously. It would be given every two weeks. Initially the treatment would take one to one and a half hours, and later the infusion would take only half an hour. Avastin acts on the blood vessels. Nausea isn't among its side effects, and it doesn't affect the blood cells. The adverse side effects could include the following:

- high blood pressure
- increased swelling in the legs
- stroke
- heart attack

In less than 5 percent of patients, Avastin could cause brain hemorrhage, abdomen perforations, and very slow healing. The cost of Avastin was relatively high (about $7,000 per month for a 70 kg person). If Avastin worked to shrink my brain tumour, I would have to take it for about six months, at an external infusion clinic (not at the LRCP). The neuro-oncologist said that Avastin was more effective than Etoposide and was effective in 20 percent of recurrent GBM tumours.

He advised us that if we were to proceed with Avastin, we should check with our health insurance provider to see if it was approved for compensation. He gave us a Roche Patient Approval form to complete that would allow Roche to help us get Avastin with compensation. The paperwork would take about two weeks to process, and Roche would mediate with my health insurance company to process the application. We needed to advise the neuro-oncologist when or if my application was approved so that he could schedule follow-up appointments accordingly.

Since I was near the one-year anniversary of my seizure, I asked my neuro-oncologist if I could resume driving again. He said that I could, but he cautioned that I shouldn't drive when I was tired or not feeling well (if I had a headache, nausea, or tingling in my limbs or fingers).

June 11, 2012—Gall Bladder Stone Attack

I woke Ivan at 2 a.m. to tell him that I had sharp pains in my chest again, just like when my gall bladder stones had caused me extreme pain. I threw up and took two Extra Strength Tylenol tablets. It felt better to lie on my side than on my back. Ivan gave me a hot bag to ease the pain. At 3:40 a.m., I threw up even more. Then I felt better and could rest more comfortably.

June 15, 2012—Follow-Up With Neuro-oncologist (More About Avastin)

At our scheduled meeting, we informed the neuro-oncologist's nurse, the resident and the neuro-oncologist about my pains on June 11. They didn't seem too concerned about them.

Ivan and I had a big decision on our hands as to the next steps. We had two options: Etoposide or Avastin. Since the neuro-oncologist wasn't too keen on Etoposide, we focused our attention on Avastin. We talked to other people about taking it and researched online using the Cancer Care Ontario website.[11] When we saw my neuro-oncologist, we still weren't sure if Avastin was the right course of action.

We informed my neuro-oncologist that my health insurance provider had verbally approved Avastin for me, but I hadn't received anything in writing.

Ivan and I took the opportunity to ask more about Avastin. The neuro-oncologist said that Avastin is a vascular endothelial growth factor (VEGF):

Vascular endothelial growth factor (VEGF) is a signalling protein that promotes the growth of new blood vessels. VEGF forms part of the

---

11 Cancer Care Ontario, www.cancercare.on.ca.

mechanism that restores the blood supply to cells and tissues when they are deprived of oxygenated blood due to compromised blood circulation.[12]

It was possible that after I took Avastin, the tumour could grow through other means. There were still lots of unknowns. For example, it wasn't known or understood what type of person was likely to be healed by it. The neuro-oncologist said that he couldn't be certain about what my brain tumour would do if I didn't opt to use another chemotherapy drug. The tumour might grow and compromise my physical and mental functions. He cautioned that some reversal could be possible after treatment, but it would depend on the extent of damage. He also told us that Avastin would impact maternity, and he strongly advised us against getting pregnant. Avastin would stay in my body for about three weeks, whereas Temodal would pass through after one day.

After much thought about the two options, Ivan and I decided that since I was asymptomatic (I was showing no adverse symptoms of cancer), I wouldn't risk anything by taking Avastin. I still needed rest during the day and wasn't on steroids to control pain. Even though my tumour wasn't totally under control, the two options did not appear ideal with the side effects and effectiveness being unknown.

It was a tough decision for us. We finally decided to wait until we had the next MRI results in July to determine our next steps for chemotherapy.

June 16, 2012—Getting Rid of Gall Bladder Stones Naturally

An online article, "How to Get Rid of Gallbladder Stones Naturally in 6 Days," was recommended to me.[13] I followed the procedure very carefully. I prepared by eating an apple a day for five days before I started the cleanse. For the cleanse, I needed to have Epsom salts, lemon juice and olive oil. The natural procedure seemed to work, and what I purged looked

---

12 Ananya Mandal, "What Is VEGF?," News Medical Life Sciences, http://www.news-medical.net/life-sciences/What-is-VEGF.aspx.

13 "How to Get Rid of Gallbladder Stones Naturally in 6 Days," eHow, http://www.ehow.com/how_4667461_rid-gallbladder-stones-naturally-days.html.

like the website photo. Fortunately, I have not had any attacks since that procedure.

July 10, 2012—MRI Scan

I had my MRI scan as usual.

July 27, 2012—Follow-Up with Neuro-oncologist— No Further Growth

I updated the nurse and neuro-oncologist that I had registered at Wellspring for further "therapy," like yoga and meditation. They had no comment.

The neuro-oncologist showed us my MRI scans from July 2012 and compared them to the results from the May 2012 scans. There was no further tumour growth in the right hemisphere; that was great news. He cautioned that my tumour was very close to the main ventricles in my brain. If the tumour continued to grow, it might affect the corpus callosum, and my left and right coordination would be compromised. He agreed that since I had no adverse symptoms, Avastin would not be necessary at the moment, but he said that continuous monitoring was still critical.

August 9, 2012—Follow-Up from Roche PAP

We received a call from the Roche Patient Assistance Program (PAP), and we advised the agent that we had chosen to not use Avastin since my tumour remained stable (not growing or spreading).

September 26, 2012—MRI Scan

I went for my MRI scan as usual. This time, the MRI machine was new. The next day, I felt pain in my right arm where the contrast dye needle was inserted.

October 5, 2012—Follow-Up with Neuro-oncologist

I updated my neuro-oncologist about the pain in my arm after my MRI. He didn't seem concerned at all. My MRI scan results of September showed no significant difference from the previous MRI. There was still no need for Avastin. My blood tests were back to normal. The neuro-oncologist suggested that I continue with Keppra as an anticonvulsant in order to avert any seizures. I still needed to rest every afternoon, and he told me to contact the LRCP clinic if my condition worsened or changed.

October 22, 2012—Another Follow-Up from Roche PAP

We received a call from PAP again, and we advised the agent that we still were choosing to not use Avastin while my tumour remained stable.

25. ONGOING JOURNEY

I CONTINUED TO EXPERIENCE HEADACHES , BUT I THOUGHT THEY WERE explainable, perhaps due to weather changes (pressure changes, extreme heat or high humidity), my menstrual period, or exhausting activities and lack of sleep. I took care to make sure that I had enough rest each day. Usually it took a few days for my energy to recover after a busy day.

I went to bed when my daughter went to sleep around eight each night, and I didn't wake up until six the next morning. I needed to sleep during the day also, in the afternoon. I believe that good rest, prayers, and watching what I ate and drank helped me tremendously to manage and balance a little energetic child and my lack of energy.

Throughout 2013, I met with my neuro-oncologist on January 21, April 26, July 29, and December 2, approximately a week or so after my MRI scans. At my appointment on July 29, he told me that my appointment frequencies could change from every three months to every four months. Ivan and I were very happy to hear that news. At least we were moving in the right direction.

Every now and again, a part of my brain enhanced, or lit up, from the contrast dye to show that the tumour was still there. The neuro-oncologist continued to suggest regular MRI scans and follow-ups to discuss the scans. If a change of course was needed, we would discuss further protocol when required.

Throughout 2014 and 2015, I continued having three more MRI scans a year and follow-up appointments with the neuro-oncologist a week or so after each scan.

As of the writing of this book, my brain tumour is still present. Every once in a while, a spot lights up on my MRI scan to show that the tumour is still active (like a volcano waiting to erupt). Until such time that my neuro-oncologist deems that my scans are stable enough, I will not be returning to my job or taking on excessive stress.

Part 2
Supplementary Information

In the following chapters of this book, I will give further details about my journey with brain cancer and motherhood. I'll provide more details to help readers further understand and "get it," and I'll explain my family's experience while I recovered from my surgeries and cancer treatments.

26. Courageous Move to London, Ontario, in 2000

Courage is what it takes to stand up and speak;
courage is also what it takes to sit down and listen.
                                        —Winston Churchill (1874–1965)

In 2000, after Ivan finished his master of science program in chemistry from McGill University in Montreal, he started job hunting. He received a call from 3M Canada in London, Ontario, asking him to go for an interview. He had interviewed at 3M before, but because he did not have a master's degree, he was not offered the position.

On this instance in April 2000, they interviewed him again. They were impressed that he had taken their feedback to heart and followed through with getting a master's degree, and they immediately offered him the position.

Ivan's new employer gave him two weeks to move to London. We had just moved into our basement apartment in January after a very long search. When we finally decided to move from Toronto to London, Ivan and I immediately started to look for a temporary place to stay for a short term. In the meantime, we would look for a permanent home. I had lived in London from 1993 to 1996, while completing my master's degree in engineering, so I felt comfortable and knew where to look for a place to stay.

After seeing several unsuitable locations in London, after 9 p.m. Ivan and I finally went to the last location on our list. We were surprised and relieved when we found the apartment to be clean and hospitable. The tenant wanted to sublet her apartment for four months, and we thought that was perfect timing for Ivan to get settled into London and get used to working at 3M.

Fortunately, the person from whom we were subletting lived in Mississauga too, and we easily obtained the apartment keys without a lot of trouble or inconvenience. We coordinated timing and eliminated the hassle of driving back and forth to get the keys.

We next told the landlords for our new Toronto basement apartment that we were moving out. We were a little hesitant to give them the news when we had only just moved in four months earlier. They were not surprised at all and were actually very happy. They said, "We didn't know when or how to tell you both that our house is now sold. The new homeowners will take possession in August." The timing was just great for us, given Ivan's short-term sublet apartment lease in London.

I gave notice to my Toronto employer that I was moving to London. The very day after I formally submitted my resignation notice to my manager, there was a big corporate announcement. All the employees in the development corporation were ushered to the 42nd floor of one of our buildings in downtown Toronto, and the news was so important that staff from the field were also brought in. It would impact all of the staff across Canada, and it had to be coordinated well so that all affected staff would hear the news at the same time.

The announcement was that our whole development corporation would be outsourced to an external service provider. Some people thought that I had good foresight to leave the company, but truly I didn't know that such big news was on the horizon. However, God knew that following Ivan to London would be in my future. Our circumstances were such that I finally wanted to be living in the same city as my husband. Since I had lived in London before, I was very excited to be moving away from a "corporate" busy downtown life in Toronto to a smaller city like London. We found that Londoners were far more polite and patient, giving others the time of day and even taking the time to hold the door open at a shopping mall. Though I really enjoyed my job and colleagues, I was happy to leave the hustle and bustle of downtown Toronto.

After I tendered my resignation, I received two job offers in London. One job offer was given to me on the spot even though I was late for the 7:45 a.m. interview because the Toronto subway and transit system malfunctioned that morning. Eventually, for security reasons, I accepted the other job offer. It's a small world in the construction and facility management industry, and I already knew my colleagues at the new job.

In the meantime, Ivan found a new detached home for us in London. He gave the realtor a conditional offer ("subject to my wife seeing and approving the purchase of the home"). The house was situated at an intersection of two streets, and the house number was 14. In the Chinese tradition of feng shui, a house number with a 4 is unlucky because "4" sounds like "death" in Chinese. We also worried that the house was located at an intersection of two streets where luck might not flow well into our home.

I called my mom and explained that the house was very nice (it was the builder's model home) but had the two problems. She said, "Pray and don't be worried."

Prior to closing the deal, we visited the Roman Catholic parish closest to our future home. The parish of St. Pius X (later renamed to Holy Family Parish) was within walking distance from our potential home; it was only about one kilometre away. We prayed at the tabernacle in the church for guidance to buy the right home and asked Jesus and His Mother Mary for protection from all evil and danger. We then felt comfortable making our final decision to purchase our first home, despite its location and house number.

We were concerned about simultaneously paying the rent for Ivan's London apartment, the rent for our Toronto basement apartment, and the mortgage payment for our new London house. We were very fortunate that the property managers of Ivan's apartment wanted to paint it before new tenants took over. They gave us a credit for two weeks' rent, which helped for our initial mortgage payment.

When this "coincidence" happened, we knew that God had answered our prayers. We felt more comfortable with our new home purchase, and we were certain that God would always watch over us.

We moved into our current home in London, Ontario, in August 2000.

27. Telling Family and Friends

True love causes pain.
Jesus, in order to give us the proof of his love, died on the cross.
A mother, in order to give birth to her baby, has to suffer.
If you really love one another,
you will not be able to avoid making sacrifices.

—Mother Teresa[14]

Ivan had the fortunate and unfortunate task to tell our family and friends about our "news."

As a very happy and proud father, Ivan delighted in announcing that our baby girl, Genevieve, was born on Tuesday, February 8, 2011, at 3:13 p.m. No more guessing sex, date, time, name, weight, etc. Genevieve was born healthy and weighed five pounds two ounces at birth. Family and friends sent us flowers, gifts, and cards to congratulate us as new parents.

Then Ivan had to add that there were "complications" during birth. I had to remain in the hospital. At the time of Genevieve's birth, Ivan just knew that I had a large mass in my brain. We didn't know if the mass was benign or malignant. It was only after we got the pathology results that we realized that our joy and excitement would be short-lived.

Ivan communicated via email to our immediate families so that everyone would get one message at the same time. We then shared my health condition with our friends, managers, and work colleagues.

Ivan's manager was extremely compassionate and told him to take his time to return to work. He knew that Ivan was a hard-working and valuable employee, and he understood what Ivan was going through because his own wife had had a brain tumour. His manager just "got it."

---

14 Mother Teresa, quoted in José Luis González-Balado, comp., *Mother Teresa: In My Own Words* (Toronto: Random House, 1996), 33.

He knew that being a new parent and a caregiver for a cancer patient at the same time would be physically and mentally taxing and tiring. Fortunately for Ivan, he still had vacation time, lieu time, sick time, and paternity leave. He was able to be home with Genevieve and me.

Ivan is a very calm and collected person who rarely shows his emotions. He told me that the initial reactions from family and friends about my brain tumour included,

- "Oh no!"
- "Oh [expletive deleted]!"
- "What now?"
- "Did I just read what I read?"
- "She's too young to die."
- "But she just had a baby."
- "Are they joking?"
- "This can't be true or possible."
- "Why... why... why?"
- "How... how... how?"
- "But... but...but..."
- and worst of all, "Deny, deny, deny."

I remember that my father asked me to get a second opinion about my diagnosis. I told him the Brain Tumour Foundation of Canada was founded right here in London, Ontario. The top medical professionals are here. Where else could I go for another opinion? I could go to Toronto, Montreal, or Calgary, but I confidently knew that my journey was to remain in London.

My father told me to pray and that everyone was praying for us. He said that it was important to believe in prayers; otherwise everyone was "wasting their time on their knees." My father was very to the point and direct on urgent matters. I knew that he was right.

The Gospel of Mark says, "Therefore I tell you, all that you ask for in prayer, believe that you will receive it and it shall be yours" (Mark 11:24). I recalled another passage in the Bible where Jesus healed a twelve-year-old girl and said, "Do not be afraid; just have faith" (Mark 5:36). My father repeated to me, "You *must* have faith in God."

After the reality set in, family and friends were more helpful. They asked more productive questions, like the following:

- When will you know your treatment schedule?
- How can I help?
- What food can I make for you?
- What will you do with Genevieve?

In time, all those questions or unknowns were answered.

28. Genevieve's Baptism Day

We didn't make any fuss for Genevieve's baptism. Had she been born around the original due date of March 7, she would have been baptized during the Easter Vigil celebration. As God would have it, Genevieve was baptized and called into God's family on Saturday, February 26.

Ivan called my family and his immediate family and invited others via email. The word spread, and cousins, aunts, uncles, neighbours, friends, and even our work colleagues came to London to be part of Genevieve's special baptismal day. It was a cold, blizzardy day. Family who rarely visited found their way to London.

Usually Ivan and I drove back to Mississauga, where both our families live, for various celebrations: birthdays, Christmas, Easter, Chinese New Year, and other special events. The extended family often asked us, "How far is London?" Lo and behold, family members who had never visited Ivan and me in London managed to find their way to our parish church.

We really didn't know how many people would show up. Our pastor kept seeing the door open and shut as more people entered for the celebration. About fifty or so people attended Genevieve's baptism. I believe our pastor was surprised to see so many people because he knew we had only finalized the baptism date and time four days earlier.

We sincerely regret that we couldn't offer a reception of food and drinks for our guests, who travelled in bad winter weather to join and support Ivan, Genevieve, and me. We learned that one of our guests swerved on the slippery highway and got stuck. She needed to be towed out. This was the life of winter in London, Ontario, which sometimes was very different from Mississauga and Toronto. London often has more snow than Mississauga.

We were very pleased to see such a large group gathering together and praying for us on Genevieve's special day.

29. Health and Travel Background

I have the feeling that we are in such a hurry
that we do not even have the time to look at one another and smile.

—Mother Teresa[15]

I WAS VERY SURPRISED TO DISCOVER THAT MY MANY YEARS OF HEADACHES AND several months of nausea and vomiting (which I thought were "normal" for pregnancy) were possibly related to a brain tumour. My sinuses were also clogged up toward the end of my pregnancy. This was also a possible sign of a brain tumour. Who with headaches, nausea, and sinus problems would ever suspect a brain tumour? I was stunned to hear that my "usual" headaches throughout my life may not have been so typical or hormone related after all. I was also utterly shocked to learn that my brain tumour (at its largest dimension) was about 8 cm, or the size of an orange.

I clearly recall telling my family doctor in London that I often threw up in hot environments. She just noted in my medical file that I had "sun sensitivity." When she referred me to an obstetrician, one of the first things I told the obstetrician was about my nausea and frequent migraine-like headaches. She also did not think the headaches were a big problem, as headaches are typical when hormones change in pregnant women.

Ivan and I like to travel to discover new cultures, languages, and foods. In 2001, my manager at work processed my expense claims and said, "You work hard and deserve a good vacation." He was an avid traveller, and he offered to find me a good price to fly to Kuala Lumpur, Malaysia (where I was born), in southeast Asia. Ivan was interested to see where I was born. We started the planning process, and I contacted my relatives to let them know that we were coming for a visit.

---

15 Quoted in González-Balado, *Mother Teresa*, 23.

After a short time in Malaysia, with its hot and humid weather, I got sick. My mouth was frothing, and it was like I had a heat stroke. I had to tell my cousin that I needed rest in the hotel and could not go to her house for dinner that night.

In 2003, a Severe Acute Respiratory Syndrome (SARS) outbreak affected people in Asia, Toronto, and other parts of the world. SARS is a respiratory illness that is highly contagious and sometimes fatal. I had changed employers that year, and Ivan and I decided to travel within North America instead of overseas. We chose to go to Las Vegas, USA. On the second day of our vacation, after leaving a cold grocery store in Las Vegas, I was heaving and throwing up in a grocery bag. I committed to drinking more water and ate dry raisin bread, which helped a lot with the nausea and heavy head.

In 2004, we visited friends in Paris, France. After a whole day of sightseeing on our own, I went from extreme heat outside to cold in an air-conditioned apartment. The result was not good—vomiting, as usual. My headache was piercing and pounding, and my head felt very heavy the whole night.

In 2005, we decided to go to see the Great Wall of China. We travelled a few days in hot weather and got into a cold air-conditioned taxi. Then I felt queasy, and when the taxi stopped, I got out and threw up in an alleyway.

In 2010, we went to Mexico City. It was a vacation that was planned with little lead time. I had to take a vacation or lose the days I had accumulated. Ivan and I decided to go to Mexico rather than taking an international flight because we were planning to take my niece to France later that year. We visited the shrine of Our Lady of Guadalupe for the first time and were really impressed with our experience and what we learned about the image of Our Lady.

There are photos in the appendix (figures 2 and 3) that I took with my point-and-shoot camera. I set it on the back of a pew in the church and used the automatic setting to take the photo of Ivan and me. In the background was the image of the actual tilma that the visionary Juan Diego wore when Our Lady gave him Her miraculous image on his cloak. Note the highlighted area of Our Lady's gown near the abdomen. I believe this was a sign to Ivan and me that I would become pregnant. We did not notice this highlighted area until I prayed to Our Lady after I was diagnosed with cancer. It was very interesting that Our Lady's abdomen was highlighted. The tilma was at least 100 feet behind us, and no flash photography was allowed near the image where visitors can get a closer look under the altar area.

We planned to take my niece, who was suffering from depression, to France later that year. She was not thrilled at the idea at first, but then we encouraged her to check websites about France. Slowly she changed her attitude, and she put together a list of places that she wanted to see. She became very excited to experience a new culture, language, and food, see historic sites, and go to Lourdes, where Our Lady appeared to St. Bernadette in 1858. There have been many healings reported at that site, and our family thought that my niece might benefit from visiting to ask for healing for her depression.

We called my friends in France, and everything was scheduled and planned. They were taking a vacation at the same time, and we were all excited about our plans. The day before we were to depart from Toronto, the Eyjafjallajokull volcano in Iceland erupted. Aviation officials closed Europe's air space for five days, out of fear that ash from Eyjafjallajokull could harm jet engines. This impacted more than 10 million air travellers and cost $1.7 billion U.S.[16]

Ivan and I were in a big dilemma, because there were few options to go to Europe. We kept our eyes on the news, hoping that the winds would change. The reporters said that the winds could change again; if we got to Europe, we might get stranded there. We really didn't want to disappoint my excited niece and put her into a deeper depression.

We prayed the rosary together, and immediately after we finished our rosary to Our Lady, Ivan's father phoned us. He told us that we should seriously think about another place to go instead of Europe. We agreed. We considered our options, and we felt that Mexico City would be a good alternative to France. It met all our needs (even though we had just visited there): my niece could experience a different culture, speak Spanish, eat

---

16 "Iceland volcano: area north of Bardarbunga evacuated," CBC News, www.cbc.ca/m/touch/world/story/1.2741422.

Mexican food, see historic sites, and also to go to Tepeyac Hill, where Our Lady appeared to St. Juan Diego in 1531. We decided to pack for France and also pack other bags so we'd be ready to go back to Mexico.

The next day, we drove to Toronto and kept our eye on the website to see if our flight to Paris was going to go. When we finally reached our flight carrier (Air Canada) by phone, they said the flight was cancelled, and the next flight to Paris would be after we had planned on being back in Canada. Ivan talked to my niece and his parents about our change in plans. They agreed that France was a "no go" and a reasonable alternative was to all go to Mexico City instead.

Ivan's father was very dedicated to Our Lady of Guadalupe. After we returned the first time from Mexico, he had many questions for us about seeing the shrine and the tilma. We knew he really wanted to see the shrine too, so we invited him and my mother-in-law to join us. My father-in-law was very happy to be joining us, to see where Our Lady appeared near Mexico City. I had read a book by Sister Patricia Proctor, *101 Inspirational Stories of the Rosary*, about miracles happening while someone prayed the rosary. We could add our story to this book.

Ivan and I were always careful to avoid the extreme heat and cold that seemed to cause my nausea and vomiting. Hindsight is 20/20. In retrospect, my brain tumour was likely present for a long time before it was officially detected by an MRI scan in 2011. The tumour was probably benign until stressful circumstances "woke it up," like saying, "Get up now!"

In the latter part of my pregnancy, the nausea and vomiting returned. The vomiting was so physically and intensely painful that I stomped my feet repeatedly while throwing up, but the stomping didn't help alleviate the burning feeling in my throat. I remember Ivan watching me heave and cry. I had thought that morning sickness only occurred in the first trimester of pregnancy, but then I read on the Internet that some women endure morning sickness throughout their whole nine months of pregnancy. After I learned that, I felt like I was not the only one suffering through pregnancy.

In the final months of my pregnancy, I also felt very congested in my sinuses. I told Ivan how "plugged up" I felt. He kept telling me to stop making a funny "squinty" face every time I got up from a sitting position.

We attended prenatal classes on Tuesday nights, and we thought we were well ahead of the other parents in our class. We thought we were prepared for everything. During those prenatal classes, Ivan pointed out every time I made a funny face. I would reply, "What do you mean?" The next time I made the funny face when I got up from sitting, he said, "There…you just did it again." I was not aware of it until Ivan kept pointing it out to me.

We missed our final prenatal class because Genevieve had already been born. Fortunately, I had read about Caesarean sections, because I thought that I should be prepared no matter what our circumstances would be. When I read about C-sections, little did I know that I would not be awake during the operation.

Our plans were for me to breastfeed our newborn. At our prenatal classes, we were given lots of information about breastfeeding and lactation, etc. We bought maternity clothes, including nice pyjamas for me to wear in the hospital after birth.

As we continued on our journey with our newborn, we realized that we were never in control. God had a bigger plan for us.

30. GENEVIEVE'S DEVELOPMENT

We cannot choose our external circumstances,
but we can always choose how to respond to them.
—Philosopher Epictetus, c. 55–c. 135 CE[17]

IVAN AND I WERE NEW TO PARENTHOOD, AND WE WERE TRULY NEWBIES. WE were on our own in London, with most of our family about two hours away.

Ivan's mom showed us how to swaddle Genevieve in a receiving blanket. Ivan was very good at wrapping Genevieve tightly so she didn't move too much. When she was really small, he held her like a football. Her head would be in his hand, and her feet were nestled in his arm.

The public health nurse recommended a very good family home visitor to us, as promised. This lady was very pleasant and helpful and knowledgeable about baby, toddler, and child development. She helped us with Genevieve's development and was a great resource for new parents. She also understood that we were also facing a terminal cancer diagnosis.

The nurse introduced us to our family home visitor on April 5, 2011. She was happy to meet us and said that the Healthy Moms, Healthy Babies program could progress at the pace that we felt was comfortable. We typically met every six weeks, and we could ask as many questions as needed.

Resource Material for Child Development

The family home visitor always brought great resource materials for us. She gave us wonderful and fun suggestions about how to help Genevieve develop her gross and fine motor skills and verbal skills and form healthy

---

17 Philosopher Epictetus, c. 55–135 CE, quoted in the movie *The Ultimate Gift*.

eating habits. She was patient and kind and always willing to make sure that we understood the materials she gave to us.

She also gave us great tools, like a laminated black-and-white sheet so Genevieve could learn to focus her eyes. She also brought great information on DVD, like how to make safe toys at home and put our baby to sleep.

Being new to parenthood, Ivan and I didn't know about the NDDS (Nipissing District Developmental Screen) checklist that our family home visitor introduced to us. This was a checklist of milestones at different points in the development of a baby, toddler, and child. NDDS also offered some suggestions for activities to do with one's child in each corresponding age group. There are checklists for up to age six available from the NDDS website, www.ndds.ca.

At the appropriate time, the family home visitor did the NDDS check for Genevieve. Ivan and I found that the list really helped us to watch for development milestones, like Genevieve being able to hold up her head while on her belly, roll, sit up steadily, cruise while holding on to furniture, and finally take her first steps. Genevieve did really well for her age and, for the most part, passed all of the milestones on the checklist.

Feeding Genevieve

Genevieve was good at burping and giving us clear cues about what she needed. She loved to slobber on her toys. We thought she would have teeth at four months, but her teeth did not cut through her gums until after her first birthday. To our surprise, her two upper lateral incisors came out first. These are the teeth adjacent to the main front teeth.

Genevieve didn't eat store-bought mushy foods from a jar. Ivan blended food for her, and she enjoyed it. She loved to eat peas, corn, and broccoli. She was not very fond of meats like chicken or beef. We needed to look for other ways to give her protein, and Ivan often made eggs for her. She really liked eating berries: blueberries were her favourite, then raspberries, strawberries, and blackberries. She also loved the sweetness of banana and liked to peel it like a monkey (from the bottom rather than from the stem). Fortunately, Genevieve had no food allergies, and that made it much easier for us to eat at restaurants.

Our Connection with the Family Home Visitor

The family home visitor was always punctual and reminded us when our next meeting would be. On August 31, 2012, we were scheduled to meet with her. She was not usually late, so after we had waited about thirty minutes, we called her office. Her message directed us to call our public health nurse.

From the nurse we found out that our family home visitor was dealing with an illness in her family and needed to take some time off. The nurse asked if we wanted a new family home visitor. We declined because Genevieve had developed a good rapport with our original one.

On December 10, 2012, our family home visitor came to see us again. She told us that her son had been diagnosed with a glioblastoma multiforme grade IV brain tumour. Because she was now a caregiver for her eldest son, she "got it" and understood what we had been going through. We shared several common health care providers. Unfortunately, her son passed away in January 2013. We learned about his death when the nurse came without the family home visitor on January 24, 2013. We were very shocked and sad. On the same day, after our meeting, we went to the funeral of her son in St. Thomas, Ontario.

Our family home visitor was a woman of strong Christian faith. We knew that it was providential; our public health nurse was guided to choose her for us because she knew our faith would help us bond quickly. We realized that the people we meet in life are not coincidences but are there for us to learn from and grow. It was simply a blessing to meet and get to know this wonderful and kind woman. We will never forget our family home visitor and all of her great advice and suggestions for us as new parents.

When I thought about her son, I realized how precious and fragile life is after someone is diagnosed with a terminal brain tumour. He had only just been married a few months earlier, and his life was lost so soon afterwards. I appreciated that everyone had their own share of suffering in life, even though on the outside, all may seem wonderfully stable.

It's easy to judge others, but often we are ignorant of the challenges they face in other areas of their lives. It's easy to prejudge but definitely not wise. We need to understand the full picture of their lives, in many other dimensions, like physical, mental, emotional, social, spiritual, and financial.

31. NANNY CARE FOR GENEVIEVE

Ivan and I decided to hire a nanny while I was undergoing cancer treatments. We talked to others who had hired nannies before, and their nannies were all from overseas. We located a Canadian search firm that could help us find a suitable nanny to take care of Genevieve and our house.

We started with a local contact person. The person's answers kept changing, so we asked to deal with the head office personnel in British Columbia.

We prepared a job profile and a list of qualifications and expectations and shared them with the search firm. They sent us resumes to review, and we shortlisted the potential candidates. We provided a list of shortlisted candidates to the search firm.

The nannies they suggested to us were indeed from overseas. We had to consider the time difference when setting up interviews. All of the interviews were done online starting August 20, 2011. We could see the candidates and they could see us too, through video conference calls set up by our Canadian search firm and the nannies' placement agency.

We prepared a set of questions about past nanny experience, qualifications for child and home care, and availability. Ivan and I noticed that most of the answers seemed very standard, and we thought that the potential nannies were coached by their placement firm.

Due to the time difference, we often had conference calls late at night on the weekends when the nannies would not be working for their employers. We eventually shortened the list further to two final candidates. We had a second interview with both candidates and then finally settled on one nanny. She was in Hong Kong at the time and needed to be released from her current employer.

After several months of waiting and obtaining approvals, etc., our nanny arrived in Toronto. We picked her up from the airport on April 25, 2012. We planned for her to stay overnight at a hotel because of the long journey from Hong Kong. The next day, we did a quick trip through downtown Toronto to show her see some major sights, like the C.N. Tower, Lake Ontario, and the central financial district, and let her change her money to Canadian currency. We then picked up Genevieve from my in-laws and drove back to London.

We bought a new bed, mattress, sheets, pillows, and door lock for the room the nanny would use in our house. We also paid for her flight to Toronto and her stay at the hotel and bought her health insurance for the three months until she would qualify for provincial insurance. We registered and paid for a first aid course for her also. We spent a lot of time planning for her arrival and making sure that she would feel comfortable living with us. We gave her a big welcome basket in red and white to welcome her to Canada, and we equipped her with road maps and bus maps so that she wouldn't feel lost in London. We also gave her the job expectations and house rules.

She wanted to go away to visit "friends" on the weekends and stay overnight. We thought that was odd because she said that she didn't know anyone in Canada. Little by little, we realized that she wasn't the right person to take care of our daughter. After the long eight-month expedited process, we let her go. She had been living with us for less than three months.

It was a difficult decision to make, given all the time and money we invested in bringing her all the way to London. We needed to make a sound decision for the future of our family, especially for Genevieve's sake. She was soon going to be moving from part-time to full-time daycare, so our concerns about her care were allayed.

32. Brain Tumour Support Group Meeting

I was anxious to attend our first Brain Tumour Support Group (BTSG) meeting at a local Baptist church in London's downtown area. The monthly meeting was organized by the Brain Tumour Foundation of Canada (BTFC). It was on the first Tuesday of the month and usually started at 7 p.m. and went until about 9 p.m.

The BTSG facilitator was very open, friendly, and welcoming. She told us to sign in, enjoy a refreshment, and find a spot on a couch or chair. Ivan and I took some refreshments and settled onto a sofa together.

Shortly thereafter, the facilitator started the meeting. Everyone was asked to introduce themselves since there were some new members, like us, who didn't know anyone. Ivan and I felt relieved that we were not the only "newbies."

Each person introduced himself or herself and gave an update on how he or she was coping with the brain tumour. The facilitator was excellent and remembered everyone's situation and tumour type. I was totally amazed, because I knew my brain was mushy. Ivan and I were happy to meet other long-time survivors with the same type of malignant tumour as I had. Meeting three men with a GBM IV tumour gave me hope and relief. I felt so much better when I heard some good news. It was therapeutic to share my own story with those who I knew "got it" because they understood what my family was going through with brain cancer. Most members were parents too, so they also understood the challenges Ivan and I faced with being new parents.

The BTSG consisted of several brain tumour patients and their caregivers (spouse, parent, older child, and so on). Some people shared long stories about how they were doing, while others were very brief and to the point. Every patient shared common feelings, and we all had a common bond—a brain tumour. There were many types of brain tumours in different areas of the brain.

When it was our turn, I explained that I was currently on treatment with chemotherapy and radiation after having had a brain tumour resection and delivering a baby on the same operating table. No one in the BTSG had ever heard of such a situation. We could tell that several members were shocked. After the meeting some members told me that I was inspirational for them. The facilitator kept remarking that I looked good for having had seventeen radiation treatments and twenty-three chemotherapy doses. I wasn't even finished my treatments yet.

Ivan and I enjoyed our first Brain Tumour Support Group meeting and finding other locals who understood what we were experiencing. Meeting "strangers" who actually knew what Temodal, Dilantin, and many other new words meant was very comforting because we didn't feel so alone. It was a good feeling to hear others "get it."

I strongly encourage any newly diagnosed brain tumour patient to seek out a support group so that they can sense the courage of others. The support group provided me with hope and courage from others who had been through similar circumstances.

The BTSG facilitator also reminded all members and caregivers about the "Spring Sprint" fundraiser that was taking place the next weekend, on Saturday, April 16 (about ten days away). The fundraiser was held annually to raise money and awareness about brain tumours.

Ivan and I kept the thought of the Spring Sprint in our minds, but we had much more to undergo before signing up for the event.

33. RAISING FUNDS FOR SPRING SPRINT 2011

THE SPRING SPRINT IS AN ANNUAL FUNDRAISER THAT RAISES MONEY FOR THE Brain Tumour Foundation of Canada (BTFC). The BTFC was founded in London, Ontario, in 1982 and is a national organization dedicated to providing hope and support to everyone affected by a brain tumour. The Spring Sprint takes place in twenty-one cities across Canada, and London is typically the first city to begin the nationwide event. Funds raised are used for the following:

- Providing programs and services which empower and emotionally support those [they] serve.
- Advocating politically and publicly for better patient care and for increased funding of brain tumour research.
- A conduit of information, raise awareness and educate the public about brain tumour issues.
- Funding research that will find the cause of and cure for brain tumours and improve patient quality of life.[18]

On April 13, two and a half days before the Spring Sprint event, Ivan registered for it and sent out emails requesting sponsorship. Our ambitious goal was $2,500, and Ivan set up as a "team" of one person. By five that same afternoon we had reached our goal. We were was absolutely thrilled and even more excited about the Spring Sprint. Suddenly we weren't feeling so silly about our "ambitious" goal. We watched our fundraising webpage fill up with many kind words of encouragement and prayers for our family.

---

18 "How You Can Help," Brain Tumour Foundation of Canada, www.braintumour.ca/626/how-you-can-help.

Our message was sent out to some family, friends, and work colleagues, who then sent our plea for donations to their own families and friends. Donations came in from our immediate and extended families and from the families of several friends and colleagues. We were overwhelmed to see so many people coming together to support us.

It was incredible how quickly and generously people responded. We were amazed to find that support came from many people we encountered through different stages in our lives: from my own current staff and co-workers, colleagues from past jobs, Ivan's work clients, hospital staff, neighbours, and even people we knew but didn't actually expect to sponsor us. The sponsors were from across Canada and all over the world, including Europe, Asia, and the United States.

On the eventful Spring Sprint day, Ivan and I proudly took Genevieve on her first stroll through Springbank Gardens in London. We had never opened Genevieve's new stroller, and we struggled to get it opened and set up. We looked like "newbie parents" in the parking lot, pushing and tugging at different straps and buttons to open the stroller. We eventually "got it" after embarrassing ourselves publicly.

I wasn't sure if I would have the energy to do the whole course. We just strolled, and before we knew it, we were at the midpoint and able to turn back. While under the Guy Lombardo Bridge, I took my chemo medication, and I continued to the end, with Ivan, Genevieve, and my parents-in-law. It was exhilarating to complete the course. The ground was wet, but the rain actually held off until our walk was completed.

Thanks to the generous support of so many people, our goal of $2,500 was well exceeded. We raised a total of $22,710 through 216 sponsors. Ivan was the lead contributor of funds by any team or individual.

Early in my cancer journey, participating in the London Spring Sprint 2011 showed my family and me how much love and support we had for my recovery. While Ivan and I were originally very concerned that our goal of $2,500 was too ambitious for two and a half days of fundraising, we realized how abundantly blessed we were with generous and caring family, friends, colleagues, and strangers too. Having committed and dedicated connections helped us in our journey.

Each year, the Brain Tumour Foundation of Canada sets up a website for their national fundraiser. We participated for the following two years, and Ivan was always the lead contributor in London.

34. MRI SCAN PROCESS

AN MRI (OR MAGNETIC RESONANCE IMAGING) SCAN USES A MAGNETIC FIELD and pulses of radio wave energy to take photos of inside your body. It is a painless process unless the individual can't stay still or is claustrophobic. The only pain is the mental anguish of being tested and finding out the results. If necessary, a contrast medium (like gadolinium) can be used, and the needle to insert the dye can be painful (but it is not a long-lasting pain). The dye helps the radiologist to see the scanned sections more clearly.

Ivan and I live about twenty-five minutes away from the London Health Sciences Centre (LHSC) or Victoria Hospital Campus on Commissioners Road, in London. It takes about five minutes to find a parking spot and walk within LHSC to get to the MRI reception area in the basement level. After winding through several corridors and waiting for the elevators, which often are full, with many patients in beds or wheelchairs also waiting to get on or off the elevators, we definitely learned patience to get through an MRI appointment.

After checking in with the MRI reception desk, Ivan and I usually proceeded to the change area, where I had to remove all metal from my body, like my watch, rings, necklaces, and eyeglasses. Metal objects can interfere with the magnetic forces of the MRI machine. I then had to put on "one-size-fits-all" hospital pants and top gown. I was given a locker in which to place all of my things and a key to ensure their security.

In the meantime, each patient had to complete a questionnaire about his or her health condition and whether he or she had had an MRI before, noting hospital location and date. The patient or caregiver also signed off his or her consent to have the MRI done.

Usually we wait for half an hour before my MRI; sometimes the wait was longer. A radiology technician usually gave me a nice warm blanket while I waited for my turn. Sometimes the technician inserted a line in my right arm so that the contrast dye could be administered more readily during the MRI scan.

Like when I had blood drawn, I always asked the radiology technician to tell me when the needle was going in. When the technician called me into the MRI room, I had to remove my eyeglasses and lie down flat on my back while foam knee props were placed under my legs. The props took the stress off my lower back while I stayed perfectly still for the next thirty minutes. I also was given earplugs to use because the machine was loud once the scan began. My head was locked into place with some open plastic guards, and I was given a panic "squeeze ball" with a button in case I had any concerns or an emergency while in the MRI machine "tunnel." The handheld device would alert the radiology technician if I pushed on the button, and the technician would stop the scan to see what I needed. It was comforting to know that I could stop the test if I was feeling unwell or claustrophobic. So far, I have not needed to push the panic button. On many occasions I felt like I needed to use the washroom, but I held off until after the scan was done.

After I was secure on the flat bed, the radiology technician pushed my bed into the MRI chamber or "tunnel." The technician then left the room and started the scan. There were loud clanking and rotating bangs, and even with the earplugs I could hear the whirring, knocking, and banging. There were stickers inside the chamber, and when I saw the characters Winnie the Pooh and Tigger, I felt like Ivan and Genevieve were with me as Genevieve's bedroom was decorated with a wall border of Winnie the Pooh and friends. (Our home builder had chosen this border without knowing that we also liked Pooh Bear.)

While the scan was ongoing, I always said a mantra, like "Jesus, Mother Mary, have mercy on me," and I repeated it again and again, just like when I underwent radiation.

After about twenty minutes, the technician returned to administer the contrast dye into my arm, which allowed the person reviewing the scan to see where the tumour was located. Since the brain and tumour were very vascular, the dye worked immediately. Some people are allergic to the contrast solution, but fortunately I wasn't. It was usually less painful when I had had a line already inserted in my arm than when I had the dye needle jabbed into me partway through the MRI scan. Most technicians were gentle, but others were more rough and strong when they pushed on my arm to prevent bleeding after the needle was taken out. On a few occasions, my right arm bruised where the needle was inserted.

There were several times when my right arm would feel numb on the day following my MRI scan. I told my nurse and neuro-oncologist, but they didn't think it was a big issue to worry about.

The MRI scan continued for another ten minutes, and then the technician returned to say, "All done." After about thirty minutes in the chamber, the noise finally stopped, and I gladly pulled out my earplugs, shed the now cool blanket, put on my eyeglasses, and returned to the waiting area to change back into my street clothes. Ivan was always there waiting patiently for my scan to be done.

The MRI scans have become routine for me now. I went from three-month-interval scans to four-month-interval scans.

Although I may be anxious to see the results, the radiology technicians cannot comment on the scans. They are analyzed by a neuroradiologist, who then sends the scans and the report to the requesting oncologist. Typically, I see my neuro-oncologist one week after the MRI scan to get the results.

35. SOUL MEDICINE PROGRAM AT LRCP

Nothing can bring you peace but yourself.
—Ralph Waldo Emerson

I SAW A COLOURFUL POSTER ON THE NOTICE BOARD AT THE LONDON Regional Cancer Program (LRCP). They were looking for women to join the "Soul Medicine" group. The colourful mandala image captured my attention. I tried many times to see the facilitator of the Soul Medicine group, but she was difficult to locate, and we couldn't find a time when we were both available.

We finally connected on August 30 to discuss the Soul Medicine program. The facilitator wanted to assess if I would be the right fit for the program. She said we would learn to "put fear second" and about our "heart line" and connection with each other and nature. We would experience feeling "timeless time," like watching a little baby sleep. I eagerly waited for the program to begin on September 14, 2011.

I was not disappointed at all. I met several women who were dealing with breast cancer for the first or second time or had other types of cancer. I was the only one with brain cancer. We were all welcomed with our different backgrounds and experiences and shared one similar bond—cancer in our own lives. It was important to maintain the confidentiality of other's physical and emotional journeys.

I learned many insights from the Soul Medicine program, like the following:

- I need to trust my own inner wisdom—be confident in myself and not worry about what others think or feel about me.
- It was important to share my own cancer journey with others who've "been there" or "done that" and really "got it" and could personally understand what I was feeling and to

know that I was not alone and that it was perfectly normal when I cried or was disappointed or angry or frustrated.

- Connecting and bonding with other women were reassuring as we had similar concerns, worries, and fears about our spouses or partners and our children and family.
- It was helpful to form a "heart line" where we felt strong with each other and were comforted by our common bond of cancer and its impact on us, our families, and caregivers.
- Synergizing with each other helped me to feel more comfortable with sharing my experience with my own life-threatening illness. While my fears and concerns were unique to me, the other women also felt similar concerns regarding the impact of cancer on their caregivers, family and friends.
- Suffering is not something we could manage on our own. We need good support and help to get through our own personal chaos in our minds and bodies.
- It was helpful to meditate and understand my fear by thinking about why I was so afraid of my cancer and the unknown.
- I realized that all we really have is this present moment.
- I realized that we cannot control the future; while all of us think we're in control of our lives, we often are not. Cancer reminded us that we were not in control at all, and that caused lots of anxiety and fear. Our replicating and abnormal cells were controlling our bodies and lives; no special treatment or "wonder" chemotherapy drug could save us, and that fear of no control scared all of us.
- We realized and had to accept that we will all die someday one way or another. No one is exempt from death. For new life to exist, death has to exist also. The cycle of life requires death to bring in new life. Life and death are the rhythm and cycle of our existence. We human beings cannot escape death. We will all die; we can never escape death— that is a certainty for everyone. While death is not

an easy topic to discuss in my culture, I realized that denying a fact of the lifecycle would only lead to profound sadness and disappointment.

- We acknowledged that nothing lasts forever.
- Creativity is a healing force. We were given blank white poster boards to create our "soulscape" using images from magazines and newspapers to create and express what made each of us feel wholesome or what spoke to our hearts.

Our Soul Medicine group met for six consecutive Wednesdays for about ninety minutes each time. I found that sharing my cancer journey in a smaller and intimate environment was extremely healing for me. Though I found the Brain Tumour Support Group very caring and compassionate, speaking in a smaller group of six women was easier, and it was more comfortable for me to share details and express my feelings more openly.

My Soulscape

For my soulscape, I cut the rectangular board into a circle to create a mandala or a circular design. I photocopied the image of Our Lady of Guadalupe and the Divine Mercy image of Jesus. Our Lady, being female, and Her Son, Jesus, being male, were clearly opposites, yet equally loving and merciful. I purposely used black-and-white photocopies as an ironic metaphor that life is not always clearly "black and white." There are always grey areas. I also copied a photo of Ivan, Genevieve, and me from August 2011.

I found my art class sketchbook from grade 13, when I was given a project to create ten pieces of work based on one single theme. Back in 1988, I always felt that time was a special and common entity to everyone. I felt somehow that my time on earth would be short. So, in ignorance of my future, in 1988 I chose "time" as the theme for my art project.

One of the black-and-white sketches that I drew was of an hourglass. Inside the hourglass, I drew (you may not believe this) a brain! I wanted the hourglass to look like a mason jar where we typically preserve

fruits and vegetables. My thought at that time was that we could preserve time and memories if we could preserve our brains. The image was
slightly cryptic and, perhaps, gross. I realize now that maybe God was
guiding me to create this image.

I photocopied my sketchbook page and added it to my soulscape
collage. All of the elements (Our Lady, Jesus, my family and sketch) were
cut into a circular shape. When I loosely placed my family photo in the
centre of the board, with Our Lady of Guadalupe, Divine Mercy Jesus,
and my brain hourglass sketch, I still felt something else was missing.

Since my soulscape was to demonstrate my life, I also wanted to
show that life is a convoluted journey and mystery. I went on the Internet and found black-and-white images of labyrinths[19] and added them to
my soulscape collage. The labyrinths were a triple spiral labyrinth, a me-
dieval labyrinth, and a chakravyutia, a threefold seed pattern with a spiral
at the centre. These circular labyrinths were perfect for my soulscape.

When I stepped back and looked at my soulscape collage (see figure
6 in the appendix), I felt very happy that my simple white board was
transformed to capture the images that I felt were important to my life:
Our prayers to Our Lady of Guadalupe and Merciful Redeemer Jesus
helped us survive my brain cancer and motherhood journey, a journey
that still continues, has many twists and turns, and ironically is never
black or white.

I kept my soulscape creation under my image of Our Lady of Guadalupe in my prayer room at home to remind me of my journey and
the importance of prayers, which contributed significantly to my overall
well-being and positive attitude toward the gift of life.

The Soul Medicine program ended on October 19, 2011. I really
enjoyed it, and I learned so much about coping with my cancer and being
a new mother.

---

19 The images were found on https://en.wikipedia.org/wiki/Labyrinth.

36. Having Good Support

By the spirit of Ubuntu—A Xhosa proverb which goes: 'Ubuntu un-gamntu ngabanye abantu.' What it means is that each individual's hu-manity is ideally expressed through his relationships with others, and theirs in turn through a recognition of his humanity. In other words, people are people through other people. That, to me, is what life means.[20]

Social and moral support came from many sources:

Good Neighbours

I mentioned earlier about our concerns regarding our house number and location. When I was diagnosed with a malignant brain tumour, my neighbours were all very supportive and accommodating.

St. Joseph's nurse Shana Da Fonseca still visits us every year near Genevieve's birthday and brings me fresh flowers. Without her astute assessment in the hospital, Genevieve and I would not be alive today. She is a true gift from God. I am always touched and amazed by her generous and giving attitude. Shana also belongs to our Holy Family Parish. What an incredibly small world! My parents-in-law say that we live in a "small town" where everyone knows each other.

One neighbour (two doors away from us) knew Shana. This neigh-bour made soup and food for my family while I was in the hospital. She understood that food is essential while we undergo a difficult crisis in our lives. We didn't have to ask for anything—she just knew that food would keep our energies up and minds alert.

Her husband helped our next-door senior neighbour too. He was very helpful when snow kept piling up and he cleared our snow with her

20 Tricia Ann Roloff, ed., *Navigating Through a Strange Land: A Book for Brain Tumor Patients and Their Families* (West Fork, AR: Indigo Press, 1994), 95.

snow blower. It saved us a lot of time and energy. We were always able to get to medical appointments on time.

Our next-door neighbour (originally from Malaysia, where I was born) knew what to cook for me and showed Ivan what to make for me. She learned from her very traditional mother-in-law and conveyed what she knew to us. In Malaysia the one-month period after childbirth is called the confinement period, and the mother and baby do not go out of the house for the whole month. Traditionally, the mom was also not supposed to bathe for the whole month. I thought—well, too late to keep to that tradition! In the hospital the nurse had helped me to bathe as soon as I could, and she told me it was good that the neurosurgeons did not have to shave my head. My hair had been divided and combed in such a way that my scalp could be peeled back for the brain surgery. I had long, thick straight black hair, and my nurse told Ivan to bring detangling shampoo to the hospital.

Our neighbour didn't follow the no-hair-washing tradition either. She reasoned that "back then" hot water was not plentiful, so women did not bathe while in the confinement period. Today, we can control our water temperature and don't need to bathe with buckets of hot water.

Ginger root was considered very important after a Caesarean section to heal the wound, and eating at least seven eggs a day was required. She didn't do that, and neither did I. I didn't want to eat eggs while I was pregnant. The thought of an egg made me feel like gagging, even though before pregnancy I liked eggs very much.

Our neighbour showed Ivan how to make sliced beef with egg and ginger. The beef was thinly sliced and took on the flavour of the ginger and sesame oil. It was very tasty, and I needed beef to get my iron levels back up to normal. I happily ate and enjoyed the egg and beef dish.

Our neighbour was very open, kind, and helpful. She truly understood the importance of healing after having a baby. She really "got it." She was very good at helping us, and she also made black chicken for my healing. A black chicken has black feathers, and its skin and meat are literally black. I ate it without hesitation because I really wanted to get better and stronger for my family's sake.

She also showed Ivan how to make bah kut teh. In Chinese, "bah" means "meat," "kut" means "bone" and "teh" means "tea" or "drink." Literally, she taught Ivan how to make "bone soup." It was common for a woman to regain her strength after childbirth by eating bone soup. She brought over large pork bones, spice mix, and cooking utensils to remove the fat and a Thermos pot that continued to cook the bone soup.

I already explained that our neighbour across our street was my chemotherapy pharmacist. I felt relieved knowing that help was only across the street.

Our next-door neighbour on the other side of our house was very gracious and kind to sit with me while Ivan and Genevieve went to church on Sundays. She was a senior and liked to talk and have someone to chat with about the "good ol' times." Out of the blue one day, she mentioned her mom. I knew that she was brought up by her grandmother but never pried to know how or when her mom passed away. I took the opportunity to ask her more about her. I clearly recall her saying very slowly, "Lin-Pei, I don't know if I want to tell you." She then said that her mom died of a brain tumour when she was very young. Back in the 1930s, her mom was diagnosed one day during the week and died by the weekend. Right there and then, I knew God gave her to us as a gift to help me through my own journey. God always knows the big picture and already knew that one day Ivan and I would live beside this well-chosen neighbour.

Good Work Friends

Friends at my work were very thoughtful when they helped us by sending cards and emails. My staff from work regularly sent handmade cards. Several staff were located in different cities, like London, Toronto, and Brantford. I know how much effort it takes to coordinate signing something as simple as a card. I appreciated their efforts in getting as many people involved as possible. I liked to emphasize the importance of teamwork, and I was glad to see that my team continued to function well together after I left.

One employee's spouse was extremely thoughtful and compassionate. His wife understood cancer and especially what was needed for the patient.

Her own beloved sister had succumbed to breast cancer, a terrible and painful disease. His wife created a kit for me to deal with my hair loss.

In the kit were two wigs that she had sewn into hats. She also gave me several hairbands with decorative pins. I could have variety in my hairstyle. She thoughtfully included coloured photos of the actual hairbands on mannequin heads. I could clearly see what she envisioned through the photos. I was very touched and emotional, happy that someone else truly understood my hair predicament and offered me easy-to-use solutions. She really "got it," and I'll never forget her thoughtful sharing of her innovation with me. It was such a beautiful and memorable gift.

When Ivan and I decided to do our first Spring Sprint in April 2011, one of my managers from a previous employer asked Ivan if he could broadcast my situation to the colleagues with whom he still kept in touch. The result was phenomenal. My work staff was extremely generous and offered to help with sponsoring us to raise money for the Brain Tumour Foundation of Canada.

Ivan's colleagues from work were also very generous in supporting us for the Spring Sprint event. One of his colleagues' parents vacationing in Europe heard about our situation and pledged. We were so amazed and touched.

As we were watching the donations coming in on our computer screen, we saw a pledge from one of Ivan's cousins in England. As it turned out, it was really one of my colleagues from an engineering firm that I had worked for twelve years earlier. He had the same name as Ivan's cousin. We finally saw the power of the Internet and how fast news could spread.

My colleague's parents also were very generous for our fundraising efforts. She obviously had kept her parents informed of my health. They were strong supporters for Ivan and me when we needed to raise funds. She also gave us lots of clothing for Genevieve because she understood that we would not have much time to go shopping while I was undergoing cancer treatments.

I also had worked with project managers on construction projects. Some project managers were easy to work with, and some were difficult. Amazingly, the ones who were difficult sponsored Ivan and me for the Spring Sprint. Here again I learned to never judge anyone too quickly.

While I was going through brain cancer treatments, a friend from a previous employer learned she had breast cancer. She encouraged me to pray, and she asked her aunt to pray also. Her aunt suggested that I forgive those I'd harmed and to pray to Jesus for healing. My friend was also very religious and prayerful, and she went through surgery strengthened by her faith and the support of her husband and son. We visited her in the hospital in Toronto, and we gave her water from Our Lady of Guadalupe from Mexico and a prayer card for healing. She's since returned to work and is doing well.

Good School Friends

Two of my classmates from university regularly visited me in London. Even though we visited each other about once a year, they made a special effort to get together more often after I was diagnosed with cancer. They took vacation days to drive from Toronto to London so we could get caught up with each other. It was always a treat to see my friends and share updates. We could talk openly about our kids, spouses, family and work issues. I always felt good after we met, and time would always slip away so easily. I felt happy that they, as dedicated workaholics too, took time off work to visit us in London.

One university friend went to Croatia and brought back a handkerchief that she touched to where Our Lady of Medjugorje appeared in 1981. I put the handkerchief under my pillow for Our Lady to know that I needed help.

The other friend's parents also supported us in raising funds for the Spring Sprint. She was usually the one to contact me, and she was the main coordinator of our meetings. This friend was always consistent in following up even though she was a very busy mom with two sons in many activities and held an important position at work.

My grade nine high school locker partner heard about my situation through social media and connected with Ivan and me via email. We finally connected by phone. She had difficult pregnancies and lost lots of blood and almost didn't live, so she understood my situation and my concern about being on the edge of death when I was diagnosed with cancer. I had not spoken to her since we graduated from high school in 1989, so it was amazing that my story travelled through social media. She graciously sponsored us for our second Spring Sprint event in 2012.

Good Family and Parish Friends

We have a very good family friend who we've known for over twenty years. When I was diagnosed with cancer he visited frequently with his daughters and brought bouquets of fresh flowers. He was born in France and really understood *la joie de vivre*, and he knew that fresh flowers always brightened my day.

His wife went through breast cancer and various treatments. Very tragically, her cancer spread quickly, and she did not live very long. Her husband and three daughters (all adopted from China) really "got it" when they came to visit us. They usually stayed for a short time because they knew that I would easily get tired.

His wife had been a special, thoughtful, and remarkable friend and teacher. She was Ivan's and my theology teacher in high school, an excellent teacher we'll always remember because of her kindness, gentle smile, and generous spirit.

My friend's mother in France was diagnosed with liver cancer, and she sent via her son a bottle of holy water from Our Lady of La Salette. When we visited France in 2004, her husband drove Ivan and me from Paris to La Salette. Her husband was well known in La Salette because he was the architect for several projects there. She knew we were faithful to Our Lady of La Salette. We were grateful that she gave us water from the shrine high up in the mountains of France where Our Lady appeared to two shepherd children in 1846, about fifty miles south of Grenoble.

My brother and sister-in-law and their young children went to France in 2011, and at every church they said a rosary and lit candles for my family. They went to Lourdes and offered masses there for us, and they generously brought back lots of holy water for us too.

One close family friend of my in-laws went to the Shrine of Rosa Mystica in New York and brought back a bottle of holy water for me. I put the water with all my holy water from Lourdes, Fatima, Medjugorje, and the River Jordan, where Jesus was baptized.

I mention only a few incidences in this book, but several family members and friends offered masses for us. We appreciated their thoughtfulness and prayers.

Many people in our Holy Family Parish continue to pray for my family, where my name is on the prayer line list. I also found out that many others in other parishes, like in neighbouring St. George Parish, were praying for my family. One day while I was at Wellspring (a place where cancer patients and their caregivers can gather to find support and healing), a lady from St. George's parish said she was praying for someone who was diagnosed with brain cancer and had a newborn. She didn't know it was me, who had been sitting right beside her for a couple of art therapy sessions.

Our pastor regularly asked us about my health status. He consistently followed up and knew when to get updates. He was very diligent and caring, and I was comfortable that he shared my news with the office staff. He was a very dedicated pastor, and I got to know the office staff, who were kind and thoughtful.

One regular Sunday parishioner saw Ivan without me at mass. After mass, she asked Ivan if his wife had slept in and could not make it. Ivan told her that I had given birth and was still in the hospital recovering from my surgeries. I was sure this lady never assumed that anyone had been sleeping in again. It was an innocent error to make quick conclusions without knowing all the circumstances.

Believing in Strangers Too

For the Spring Sprint event in April 2011, we got sponsorships from people who were strangers to us. We believe that one of their family or friends who knew us shared our invitation to sponsor us for the walk. We are truly thankful for their financial, spiritual, and moral support for the Brain Tumour Foundation of Canada and for my family.

37. Anti-Cancer Foods

We got lots of recommendations from family and friends about what to eat and what to not eat. The spice turmeric with black pepper was said to control cancer, and Ivan was happy to make me lots of different kinds of curries with turmeric. He is a chemist by training, so naturally he loved to mix different ingredients together.

My father was always checking on the Internet to find healing foods to eat. He would send emails on whatever he found to all my siblings and their spouses, nieces, and nephews. Ivan was on the distribution list also and followed my father's emails to try various foods like tomatoes, mushrooms, garlic, and ginger. Ivan also bought several books to find recipes for me.

Anti-Cancer Food References

Ivan found several books with healthy cancer-fighting remedies to help me heal and cookbooks that provided recipes that included many anti-cancer ingredients. Detailed publishing information about these books can be found in the reference list at the end of the book.

The Scientific American book *What You Need to Know About Cancer* talks about how cancer develops, cancer detection, improving conventional therapy, future therapies, and living with cancer.

Another helpful book was from *Reader's Digest*: *Food Cures: Breakthrough Nutritional Prescriptions for Everything from Colds to Cancer*. This book lists various foods that can remedy common issues like headaches, migraines, menstrual problems, nausea, colds, and flu. Recipes were included to help the readers to incorporate the healthy ingredients into their diet.

Reader's Digest has another book, *Foods That Harm, Foods That Heal: the Best and Worst Choices to Treat Your Ailments Naturally,* which discusses nutrition, with an A-to-Z guide that says whether particular foods heal or harm us and a food guide of what to eat for various ailments.

The 150 Healthiest Foods on Earth: The Surprising, Unbiased Truth About What You Should Eat and Why, by Jonny Bowden, discusses vegetables, grains, fruits, dairy, meat, poultry, eggs, fish, seafood, oils, sweeteners, and more in sufficient detail for the reader to understand the usefulness of the food for health. It also lists the "Experts' Top Ten" for each type of food; this list is a summary and very easy to understand.

A book by Richard Béliveau and Dennis Gingras, *Foods That Fight Cancer: Preventing Cancer through Diet,* describes their findings in three parts: Part 1: Cancer: a formidable enemy; Part 2: Nutraceuticals: foods that fight cancer; and Part 3: Nutratherapy: day-to-day. The authors say that fresh blood or angiogenesis is the key to fight cancer, and cancer can be prevented through diet. They explain that phytochemicals are the anti-cancer cocktail for our foods to prevent cancer, and key foods like the cabbage family, garlic, onions, soy, turmeric, green tea, berries, Omega 3s, tomatoes, citrus fruits, grapes, red wine, and 70 percent cacao chocolate can help prevent cancer. The authors also discuss the advantages of eating food instead of food supplements. While taking a supplement or "magic pill" may seem to be a convenient way to get all the necessary anti-cancer benefits, eating the actual food is a superior and more effective way to prevent cancer cells from developing and growing.

A book I found very interesting was written by Dr. David Servan-Schrieber, a French researcher who also had brain cancer. Ultimately, he said that eating a balanced, colourful, and healthy diet will help us to avoid cancer.[21]

After taking the chemotherapy drug lomustine, I noted that the following steps seemed to work for me. About two to three days before taking chemotherapy,

- I drank lots of clear liquids (like water and light broth).
- I cleared my stomach of excess food.
- I ate plain foods like congee with some meat.

---

21 Refer to the website Anticancer: A New Way of Life at www.anticancerbook. com for more details of Dr. Servan-Schrieber's findings.

- I ate soup with wontons and turmeric and black pepper.
- I ate fresh salad with chicken and a squeeze of lemon.
- I limited junk food like chips and chocolate.
- I ate whole wheat and fruits.
- I detoxified or cleansed my body to limit the nausea.

Ivan was always eager to make sure that I ate as much anti-cancer food as possible. He would switch food around so I didn't get bored of the food he prepared or cooked. I enjoyed all his curries, made always with turmeric and black pepper. Even when Genevieve was in my belly, she liked Daddy's curry and would kick to let me know she liked it. When I recently told Genevieve that she did this, she laughed and laughed because she too likes her daddy's cooking.

Ivan bought special bowls for me to enjoy my soup in. He didn't want me to get tired of eating the same thing. He is a good cook and can make something delicious from whatever we have in the fridge. He is creative and makes all his food with lots of love and care. When he has time, he also likes to present his food like the professional chefs do on television, so that it is appetizing.

Needless to say, Ivan and I learned a lot about anti-cancer foods. Ivan cooked frequently to incorporate the following list of ingredients into our family's meals:

- berries—blueberries, cranberries, strawberries, blackberries, raspberries, goji berries (eaten plain, in desserts or soups)
- grains—oats, whole wheat bread, brown rice (in breakfast, snacks, lunch or dinner), limited white breads and white rice
- honey—manuka honey (in drinks)
- meats—chicken, limited beef, pork, ox tail (in main course or soup)
- mushrooms—button, enoki, oyster, shitake, wood ear (with egg for breakfast, in soups, or as a side course)
- nuts—almonds, walnuts (in salads or snacks)
- roots—lotus root (in soups)

- spices—black pepper, cinnamon, cloves, coriander, garlic, ginger, mustard, nutmeg, saffron, turmeric, in main course dishes or side dishes (Ivan's mom makes a delicious dish called biryani; it has lots of saffron and many antioxidant ingredients.)
- vegetables—asparagus, arugula, bok choy, broccoli, spinach, yu choy (in salads or soups)
- drinks—fresh green tea made with ginger slices and honey (I had three glasses a day during my treatments), lemongrass tea (from fresh lemongrass stalks with no sugar added), soursop drink, room temperature water, and limited intake of alcohol, pop, tea, coffee and sweetened drinks

This list is not exhaustive. The reader can appreciate how much creativity Ivan used to make every meal full of essential vitamins, minerals, nutrients, and antioxidants so that my tumour would not continue to grow. Genevieve and my parents-in-law enjoyed Ivan's food too. Having anti-cancer food at any age is a bonus for everyone's health and well-being.

38. Wellspring—Cancer Care Centre

My inspiration…is based in acknowledging that in life, cancer or no cancer, we all share a fundamental common experience of suffering, of stress, of resistance to change, of a struggle in our lives to grow and learn. We all share the fear of sickness and the fear of death and the fear of losing loved ones.[22]

Wellspring is an organization where cancer patients and their caregivers can find programs like meditation, yoga, art therapy, t'ai chi, and qi gong. Wellspring provides a supportive and comfortable place to gather with other cancer patients and their caregivers. Their website contains more information about their approach, programs, and schedules: www.wellspring.ca.

Meditation

After one year of not being allowed to drive, I decided to go back to Wellspring, which was now co-located with the YMCA facility in downtown London. I went to my first meditation session on July 18, 2012, and learned about "metta" (or loving kindness) meditation.

We meditated on the following:

- ourselves
- someone else, like family or friends
- the group gathered at Wellspring
- all living things on earth

---

22 Rob Rutledge and Timothy Walker, *The Healing Circle: Integrating Science, Wisdom and Compassion in Reclaiming Wholeness on the Cancer Journey* (Halifax, Nova Scotia: The Healing and Cancer Foundation, 2010), 24.

And we repeated,

- May I be safe.
- May I be happy.
- May I be healthy.
- May I be peaceful.

We also did visualization meditation while the facilitator slowly read aloud in the dimly lit room. Her reading was very descriptive, and the words made us feel, touch, and live the images in our minds. I enjoyed the meditation session and went back again the following week.

The meditation facilitator was excellent and very calm. She made listening very easy. She was very well composed and had a gentle voice.

Art Therapy

I signed up for Wellspring on the recommendation of a peer from my Soul Medicine group on October 31, 2011. She liked art therapy and invited me to join the group. I recall that my first art therapy project was to paint something about the fall season. As we walked into the building adjacent to the Wellspring main house (prior to it moving to its current location at the YMCA), the art therapist found a fallen tree branch with crisp brown and green leaves still attached. She picked it up and said that the branch could be our inspiration for the day.

Each art therapy session began with the art therapist's introduction of a theme or thought about what we could create by either painting, sketching, sculpting, or drawing with whatever medium we chose. I found that the art therapy resources were abundant. The media included water colours, water colour pencils, oil pastels, acrylic paints, colour pencils, markers of various sizes, and different grades of paper. There were many types of brushes (small and large) and palettes, and the supplies were bountiful. We also had lots of sparkly paints and beads. I felt like I was in a heavenly art store and all was freely available to explore. The art therapist also invited participants to be free to do whatever they wanted to do. They did not necessarily need to follow a particular suggested theme.

I always enjoyed art and being creative. For my first art therapy creation I did a combination oil pastel and water colour. As with many first timers, I didn't like what I created. I enjoyed the process of creating and painting after such a long absence (twenty-two years), and I realized that there was no right or wrong in art therapy. My creation was personal and meaningful to me, and others may have interpreted my creation differently from my intentions.

After we made our creations, the art therapist offered us the opportunity to explain what we were making and our feelings about them. Often we would comment or express our own views (in a non-judgmental way) about each other's creation to lend further insight. I always found art therapy fun and happy. I enjoyed the discussions while creating and sharing at the end. Since there is no "right" or "wrong" in art, I felt very liberated and free to do what I wanted. At that time, I was still dependent on my husband to drive me (because of my seizure), and I didn't spend too much time afterward mingling and chatting with the other art therapy participants.

After I gained independence to drive again, I went back to Wellspring to sign up for more sessions. I enjoyed art therapy because the freedom to create anything felt so good. Art took my mind away from suffering and problems, and I enjoyed talking with other cancer patients and caregivers during the sessions.

I also found it very therapeutic to laugh while creating something, sometimes arbitrary and sometimes very thoughtful and meaningful. Even when we knew we made a mistake (like dripping paint on a spot that we did not intend to paint), the art therapist always encouraged us to explore where the universe was taking us. Often, the universe showed us more amazing things than we could ever have imagined at the outset.

Our creative styles varied each week because we used different media and were given different starting points. Our end product could reflect a realistic scene or an abstract scene. There was nothing prescriptive about art therapy; this felt so good after being prescribed chemo after chemo with side effects. It was truly liberating for my mind and soul to feel completely free of constraints.

For a sampling of my creations from art therapy, see figures 7 to 11 in the appendix. I gravitated to creating circular designs (or mandalas).

A circle has no start or end, and a mandala is a therapeutic image for me. While life began, it does not last forever, and then a new life begins again; to me, a circle represents life and its endless continuity.

As my art therapist reminded us, "Art therapy can be a life force." It involved a wholesome approach of using our tactile, emotional, cognitive, and spiritual gifts and talents. We expressed our creations in a safe space, knowing that our thoughts were personal and unique but could also be common to other art therapy participants.

As I would later learn and appreciate better, art therapy is effective in healing the mind and body. It was therapeutic because we created a third-party relationship. The three parties were me, the other people— other participants and the art therapist—and my creation. I found it easier to express myself and talk about my issues and feelings through what I drew, painted, or coloured. Our creations were a strong means to express our thoughts and emotions through various colours, shapes, textures, and brushstrokes.

I always enjoyed art therapy; it made me feel like I managed to create something, even though we had only 1.5 hours to develop a concept and complete the finished product. There was no time to sketch any details in pencil and refine the artwork. We worked very randomly and didn't worry about perfection. Art therapy was all about expression and being able to convey our feelings and emotions through our creations.

Yoga

After July 2012, when I had the freedom to drive myself again, I signed up for yoga on Tuesday and Thursday mornings. I really enjoyed yoga. It brought my mind and physical body into balance, especially when I really needed calm and relaxation.

The Wellspring yoga instructors were excellent and knowledgeable resources too. The pace of the yoga exercises was very personal. The instructors always reminded participants to listen to their own bodies. It was very reassuring to know that we were all there to enjoy group therapy on our own merits. There was no sense of competition as far as who could be the most flexible or make the perfect pose. I didn't feel incompetent when the instructors advised me not to do the "downward facing dog" or the full "child's" pose. I needed to keep my head above my heart. I didn't want to "feed" my tumour with more blood or, worst of all, feel faint from a "head rush" (if I moved too quickly, changing from one direction to another). The instructors were very compassionate and helpful. They watched to make sure that we didn't do a pose that could cause us pain or injury. They also helped us to adjust our poses when needed. The yoga instructors just "got it." They were well experienced, having worked with many cancer patients.

Yoga reinforced the importance of breathing. Though we breathe all the time, long, slow, deep breaths are so much more calming than anxious short, shallow, and rapid breaths. Conscious breathing in and out of our noses (rather than our mouths) helped us to calm down and ground our bodies to the earth. Occasionally we would take a "cleansing" breath and sighed loudly out of our mouths instead of our noses.

Yoga helped me to "quiet my mind" and de-stress. There were always so many things to do and accomplish every day. I realized that my mind was always busy thinking about the things to do and problems to solve. After I stopped going to work, I had a lot fewer "to-dos." Calming my mind through yoga breathing helped me to relax more easily and to recover my body, mind, and soul.

Through yoga I learned about *ahimsa*—non-violence or loving kindness—and how that attribute is so important in our lives. Mahatma Gandhi was a good example of ahimsa when he said, "Be the change you want to see in the world." Mother Teresa of Calcutta also was an excellent example when she said, "If you judge people, you do not have time to love them." In yoga, we were encouraged to avoid judging ourselves or others. We just noticed and became more aware of what we were thinking and our inhaling and exhaling breaths.

One of my favourite yoga exercises was captured in one paper called, "Eight Ways To Move Chi, taught by Zen Buddhist teacher Edward Espe Brown." Each movement had a corresponding inhale or exhale. I always felt rejuvenated after doing a series of these movements. We consciously breathed in or out with each movement, which felt so natural and required little mental thought.

Yoga taught me great lessons in keeping balance. Life was truly a balancing act to manage my own and my family's, friends', and work's expectations. Whatever moves we did on one side of our bodies, we also did on the other side. For example, after we worked to stretch one leg it would be longer than the other, so we balanced ourselves by stretching the other leg too.

Yoga exercise also reinforced the importance of being in the present moment. I knew that I could not control what had already happened in the past. Also, I could not be certain that there would be a tomorrow. All I had was the present moment. I could be certain of today and that very moment. So I refocused my energy on the present moment and stopped thinking about "what if's." My thoughts and thinking shifted radically to take on the "be present now" mindset.

T'ai Chi and Qi Gong

I also signed up for t'ai chi on Wednesdays and qi gong on Fridays. I enjoyed the flow and moving energy. Through yoga, t'ai chi, and qi gong, I learned about *chi*, or "life energy force." T'ai chi involves slow and gentle movements. We learned the "short yang style" of t'ai chi and followed twenty-four moves that were condensed from the full eighty-eight movements. The movements took a lot of coordination and focus between the two hemispheres of my brain that controlled my hands and feet.

I enjoyed the slow movements to pull in or push out chi in my body. I especially liked the warm-up movement of "grinding the stone" where my legs were steady (one forward and the other behind, and feet at hip width apart). I moved my hips in a circular motion while my arms moved forward and back in a horizontal circular motion, like I was grinding corn with a flat stone. The instructor said that soon we would feel more attuned to our surroundings. Indeed she was right; I would feel my long hair drop on my arm and became obsessed to find the hair and move it off my arm.

All the programs I joined at Wellspring helped me to heal my body, mind, and soul. The programs were led professionally and were fundamental to my overall healing process.

39. Memorable Wellspring Events

Too often I see people who awaken to life and finally take care of themselves only when they are told they have a life-threatening illness. So don't spend your life dying. Live!

—Bernie Siegel[23]

SEVERAL PEOPLE IN MY LIFE LIKED TO SAY, "I WISH I DID…" OR "I WANTED TO *but*…." I could never understand people who didn't take control of their own lives. I always lived with no regrets. I did what I really loved to do and did not let anyone put me down.

Through Wellspring, I participated in events that I would never have expected to bring such rewarding satisfaction to me.

Art Panels for St. Joseph's Hospital

In two art therapy sessions, four ladies painted on clear plastic panels with acrylic paint. The panels were painted in the summer months of 2013 and were to be installed at the St. Joseph's Hospital Breast Care Clinic. On December 4, 2013, the panels were celebrated at the Norton and Lucille Wolf Breast Care Centre, where patients waited to be tested or to receive their breast exam results. We all painted about a common theme of love even though initially our styles and colours were very different.

I started with a circular form like a mandala and continued my pattern around and around, using only gold and metallic purple paint, to represent eternity or the cycle of life. It was very meditative to concentrate on the painting while repeating the patterns that consisted of many symbols, like a cross for faith, hearts for love, radiating lines for energy, thorn lines for suffering, teardrops for sadness when receiving negative

23 Bernie Siegel, *101 Exercises for the Soul: Simple Practices for a Healthy, Body, Mind & Spirit* (Novato, California: New World Library, 2005), 71.

results, and butterflies for hope. As a final touch, I added the word "love" in several languages: English, French, Italian, Spanish, Chinese, and symbolically a heart to capture all other languages. Cancer did not discriminate due to the ethnicity or culture of the person. Enduring cancer was a unique and painful journey of mental and spiritual growth, and after some time I realized how much better I was as a person (in a spiritual, physical and psychological sense).

I finally titled my painting "Loving Eternity" (see figure 11 in the appendix for an image of the panel).

Our panels were featured on a local TV news channel and the St. Joseph's website and in the magazine *Vim & Vigour* (summer 2014 issue) and the local newspaper *London Free Press* (Monday, December 9, 2013). Other websites also featured our collaboration between Wellspring and St. Joseph's Hospital.

It was exhilarating to see our paintings being recognized by others, especially those who didn't see art therapy as a means of healing for the mind, heart, and soul.

Labyrinth Project

In November 2012, Wellspring invited members to walk a labyrinth at St. Andrew's Church in downtown London. A labyrinth is used as a meditative tool and has only one entrance and one exit. Unlike a maze, which has several blocks, the labyrinth was a smooth, unobstructed circuit. There were candles lit in the darkened hall and calm relaxing music playing in the background as we individually walked through the labyrinth path.

A facilitator guided us through the labyrinth. We privately set out our own intention before starting the walk. When we got to the centre, we paused to reflect again on our intention. At the centre of some labyrinths, there are "petals" that corresponded to the following realms (depending on the size and style of the labyrinth):

- rock and mineral
- plant
- animal

- human
- angels
- divine

I enjoyed walking the path of the labyrinth that was based on the one in the Chartres Cathedral in France, which dates back to 1215–1221.[24]

My two yoga instructors from Wellspring were inspired to create a portable labyrinth. On Saturday, April 5, 2014, several Wellspring members and friends joined together to raise money to buy materials to create a painted fabric floor labyrinth. We did yoga in their studio and did a "finger" walk on a labyrinth printed on one sheet of 8.5x11" sized paper. We successfully raised sufficient funds to buy canvas, paint, paint brushes etc., to create the floor labyrinth.

The pattern of the labyrinth was drawn in pencil on off-white coloured canvas sections by someone who had experience in making portable labyrinths. Petitions and prayers were initially written by Wellspring members in pencil. Paint would later be applied over the writing. On July 25, 2014, eight people gathered to paint the labyrinth in the yoga studio. Soft, relaxing music played in the background while we concentrated on painting the lunations (curved sections on the edges) and the path edges. We used a beautiful purple latex paint, and the painting took about six hours to complete.

Our inaugural labyrinth walk took place after lots of coordination on November 18, 2014. A photo of the labyrinth is shown in the appendix, figure 12. I enjoyed walking the labyrinth. I reflected and felt very happy and proud to have contributed to the Wellspring Labyrinth Project. I felt that many members would benefit when they walked the labyrinth. The whole project was a great blend of my passion for art and meditation. My hope was that Wellspring members would appreciate and treasure the labyrinth by using it often.

The labyrinth project was featured in the local London newspaper on April 10, 2014 (*LFP West London Neighbours*). It was truly a collaborative project that resulted in many people enjoying their meditative walk.

---

24 "The Chartres Cathedral Labyrinth—FAQ's," Labyrinthos, http://www.labyrinthos.net/chartresfaq.html.

Wellspring's 10th Annual Walk

Ivan, Genevieve, and I participated in the Brain Tumour Foundation of Canada's Spring Sprint walk in April for three years. We always came through as the top fundraisers. We were so proud and happy with our generous sponsors.

In September 2014, Ivan and I decided to do the walk to raise money for Wellspring, which relies solely on donations and philanthropy to support its programs and activities. We pitched our plea to family and friends, and again they gave generously. We raised the most for Wellspring and were happy to help their efforts to raise money for its excellent and fruitful programs for cancer patients and their caregivers. We walked five kilometres in the rain and saw the sun finally come out in our last 100 metres.

Life is truly wonderful—rain or shine!

40. THE SERENITY PRAYER

God grant me the serenity
to accept the things I cannot change
Courage to change the things I can
Wisdom to know the difference.
>   —Reinhold Niebuhr (American theologian)

I WAS INTRODUCED TO THE SERENITY PRAYER WHEN I WAS IN GRADE 7. MY teacher at the time put the prayer like a banner across the top wall of our classroom. We would pray the Serenity Prayer every day. When I was thirteen years old, I did not realize how this powerful prayer would impact my life and how I would approach difficult situations. I did not completely understand the meaning of the prayer.

Later, I realized that the Serenity Prayer taught me to accept things as they are. I often said, "It is what it is." Though this sounded like a statement of resignation, I also knew that I could not change the past or what I might have done to cause my brain tumour to grow so large.

Acceptance was very important for me to be able to move on with my terminal cancer diagnosis. After acknowledging that I could not change the past, I knew I needed to focus on the *present*. I needed to focus on feeling better, rather than wallowing in self-pity. I needed to focus on being a good wife and mother. When death was knocking at my door, I knew that I had to focus my priorities on the truly important people and things in my life.

Although I often thought about the Serenity Prayer as an adult, I didn't know its power or significance. In the following three incidents, this Serenity Prayer was critical in my life.

How I Got into Civil Engineering

The Serenity Prayer helped me when I finished high school in 1989. I was hoping to go into the school of architecture at university. I was very disappointed and shocked when my high marks in math, sciences, and art and my artwork portfolio did not qualify me to get accepted into an architectural program in Ontario.

I was extremely disappointed when I received my rejection letter. I started wondering why my high marks and portfolio were not good enough. I was not so disappointed when I learned that the faculty of engineering at the University of Toronto (U of T) was accepting me into their electrical engineering program. At that time, getting into electrical engineering was a tough and competitive feat to achieve. I knew my marks were good enough, and I realized that my art portfolio was probably lacking in creativity.

I knew that I was not interested in electrical engineering as a subject or career. My sister's friend, a working architect, suggested that I consider civil engineering instead. I looked into it further and realized that architects often worked closely with civil engineers. I should have known that, but later I realized that "once a door closes, a window opens."

My new window of opportunity was now focused on civil engineering. U of T Engineering agreed that I could enter their civil engineering program because I had already qualified for their more demanding electrical engineering program.

On the first day of my orientation week at U of T, I saw a friend whom I had met in Rome, Italy, two years earlier. At the time, our school board invited all the high school students to spend a few weeks in Rome for summer school. I took art that summer, and my friend, who was from another high school, took another subject. When we re-connected, I learned that she had just finished her first year of civil engineering at U of T. She willingly offered to give me her notes and exams. I didn't know how gruelling university (especially the engineering program) would be to pursue. I definitely appreciated all the help I could get.

We attended approximately thirty-five hours of classes and tutorials every week. The homework, assignments, and projects were on top of the thirty-five hours. The notes and exams from my friend "who got it" were like a gift from God. She understood that having past notes and exams were a key to surviving engineering.

After I settled into U of T, I had to accept that I was not going to graduate as an architect. I realized later on that my skill set and abilities were more aligned to an engineer than an architect. I am sure that God knew the gifts He had given me, and He steered me back onto the path of His will.

In December 1989, the year that I entered engineering, a tragic incident occurred at the engineering school Ecole Polytechnique in Montreal where a lone gunman murdered fourteen female students and injured fourteen other people. I clearly remember sitting in U of T's convocation hall (where we would graduate four years later) to commemorate those who were murdered and wounded in the senseless event in Montreal.

It took courage to join the field of civil engineering. A majority of the students were from Italian backgrounds. My first engineering job was as a construction site project manager. The Italian that I had learned in elementary school helped me to converse with an Italian site superintendent. This helped me a lot to be on a level playing field with "the men" because I could (somewhat) speak their language and I could recognize the bad words too.

Being a female in a male-dominated field definitely took courage. In my civil engineering graduating class of eighty-four students, I was one of eleven females, which equates to being in a 13 percent minority in one engineering class. I believe that other programs, like chemical engineering, had a higher ratio of males to females, like 50:50, during my time at U of T.

A Very Rewarding Job

In 2003, I had just hired a new employee. She seemed very enthusiastic, but realistically the job was very stressful and burdensome for her. I realized that when she didn't seem to be very lucid when I called her. At this particular job, we worked from our homes and travelled to various client sites. She seemed a little dazed and incoherent, and I worried about her. I knew it was time for me to change employers, but I felt very guilty leaving a new employee who seemed so lost. I talked to her about it before I left my job. She seemed to understand my reasons for leaving. She told me not to worry and said she appreciated that I spoke to her before leaving the company.

Three years later, after returning from a vacation to visit my sister in Winnipeg, I found a handwritten note in my home mailbox from this woman. Since we had been home-based at the time, she knew where I lived. She thanked me for hiring her, and she wrote that she had found a new spiritual direction in her life.

She left me her phone number, and I called her back to say that I received her note. We decided to meet up for coffee, even though I did not drink coffee, as it caused me to have headaches and pimple break-outs.

We met up one cool, breezy, dark evening in August and had a wonderful time sitting outside and catching up. She told me that I had literally saved her life when I hired her. She wouldn't have had treatment covered for her alcoholism. I realized then that she was probably drunk when I had called her the day she seemed incoherent. I was happy that she admitted her need and sought help for her problem. She was very grateful that the company had good health benefits. The job gave her the chance to get help and be rehabilitated.

I had bought a Serenity Prayer card while I was in Winnipeg. Since this woman mentioned in her letter that she had a "spiritual awakening," I brought out the Serenity Prayer card from my pocket and gave it to her. I had bought the prayer card because it had so much meaning for me, but I didn't know at the time what I'd do with it.

She looked at the prayer card and then said, "How did you know?"

I replied with a puzzled look, "What do you mean? How did I know?"

She asked again, "How did you know?"

I really wasn't sure what she meant, so I asked, "What do you mean? How did I know *what*?"

She answered, "This prayer is said at the start of every Alcoholics Anonymous meeting."

I admitted that I wasn't aware of the significance of this prayer, and I then realized how appropriate the prayer card was for her.

We enjoyed a wonderful and tear-filled get-together. I was very happy to see that I had made a difference in this woman's life. It was such a rewarding feeling to know that I had positively changed someone else's life. It took courage for her to acknowledge her drinking problem. She was working to resolve it, and her work and family life were slowly improving. I felt so good to reconnect with her.

Though we admitted to each other about our apprehension to meet up, it was such a great leap of faith to see each other again. I had no regrets about the meeting.

Sharing the Prayer with Others

Through Wellspring's art therapy program, I met a young lady who was recovering from multiple surgeries. She was often angry and full of dark thoughts. At first, she always painted in red and black to represent her feelings.

One day I asked her if she knew the Serenity Prayer. She said, "Yeah, yeah. I know that prayer." As the weeks went by, I decided to personally write out the prayer for her and give it to her as a gift.

As a teenager, I taught myself calligraphy from reading library books. I thought I would be creative and write the prayer in my best calligraphy and frame the prayer for her. While I looked it up on the Internet to make sure that I had accurately written it, to my surprise, I found a prayer that read,

LORD, grant me the
Serenity to accept the
Things I cannot
Change, the courage to
Change the things I
Can, and the wisdom to
Hide the bodies of
Those people I had to

Kill because they
Pissed me off.

I stuck the little comic prayer on one side of a card, and on the other side I wrote the actual Serenity Prayer in my best calligraphy. I put the card in a frame and happily presented the gift to her at an art therapy session. I asked her if she would read the prayer on both sides out loud, so that the other members could see the humour and seriousness of the prayers. This Wellspring member was very happy to receive my gift. She said that she put the prayer in a prominent place in her home to remind her of the two special prayers.

Not long after, she talked about things she had learned to accept in her life. Her paintings in art therapy were done with bright colours, no longer black and red but full of hopeful colours like yellows, light green, and blue. For a few weeks, her paintings were about "past, present and future" and her family. Perhaps it was the Serenity Prayer that made a difference. Not long after her change in attitude, she returned to work.

I learned that God's plan for me was amazing. The people I encountered in my life's journey reappeared just when I needed them. God is truly an awesome God—all-knowing and all-powerful.

41. Helpful Resources

People are not disturbed by things, but by the view they take of them.
— Philosopher Epictetus, c. 55–135 CE

I liked to feel in control of my life, especially after my cancer diagnosis. I needed to know as much as I could about my brain cancer, how it developed, causes of the cancer, treatments, foods, therapies, etc. I read as much as possible online and from the books available from the Brain Tumour Support Group meetings, the London Regional Cancer Program (LRCP) library on the basement level of Victoria Hospital and the Wellspring library and those recommended by friends. I wanted to learn more about brain cancer and healing.

The following books were helpful in my information gathering and may help the readers to "get it."

One of the first books I borrowed from the LRCP's library was *Musing and Muttering…Through Cancer* by David Gast. Gast endured several forms of cancer and always remained faithful to his Christian faith. He cited many verses from the Bible to explain his cancer journey and recovery.

Henri Nouwen was a Roman Catholic priest. He wrote about the "cup of suffering" that Jesus Christ endured. I found his insightful book *Our Greatest Gift: A Meditation on Dying and Caring* very thought-provoking, and I took away a key message:

> *The real question before our death, then, is not, How much can I still accomplish, or How much influence can I still exert? but, How can I live so that I can continue to be fruitful when I am no longer here among my family and friends? That question shifts our attention from doing to being. Our doing brings success, but our being bears fruit. The great*

paradox of our lives is that we are often concerned about what we do or still can do, but we are most likely to be remembered for who we were.[25]

Ivan and I often sent our nieces and nephews postcards from the places we had visited. My sister's family called us the "gypsies" because we like to travel around the world. My young niece couldn't remember to say "gypsies" so she called us the "Egyptians" when we visited them.

In retrospect, my niece was quite correct to call me an Egyptian. I felt like I was spending a lot of my time planning for my death and funeral. After I knew that my tumour had spread from the left hemisphere to the right, Ivan and I visited with our pastor to find out the funeral protocol at our parish. From a long time back (before the cancer diagnosis), whenever I heard a hymn that I liked at mass, I would whisper to Ivan that I would like that song for my funeral mass. He thought that I was morbid to think about death. After the mass I jotted down the name of the song so that I wouldn't forget. When it came time to consolidate all my notes, I found I had many songs to choose from. I felt like a real Egyptian, as they were historically known for spending their lives preparing for their death.

The books by Immaculée Ilibagiza with Steve Erwin describe her spiritual, mental, and psychological transformation during the genocide in Rwanda, Africa, in 1994 when at least 800,000 Rwandans were slaughtered in approximately 100 days. Her book about the rosary captures how she came to love Our Mother Mary and learned to say all the mysteries of the rosary.

Ilibagiza's book about Our Lady of Kibeho explains the apparitions of Our Lady to special visionaries in Rwanda. Our Lady told the Rwandan visionaries to share her message to "not forget that God is more powerful than all the evil in the world…the world is on the edge of catastrophe."[26] Our Lady gave the visionaries images of a country full of slaughtered people; the visions were horrid and "rivers ran thick with

---

25 Henri Nouwen, *Our Greatest Gift: A Meditation on Dying and Caring* (New York: Harper Collins, 1994), 38.

26 Immaculée Ilibagiza, *Our Lady of Kibeho: Mary Speaks to the World from the Heart of Africa* (Carlsbad, California: Hay House, 2008), 150.

human blood."[27] This book detailed "the Rosary of the Seven Sorrows"[28] and identified the prayers Our Lady gave to the visionary (Marie Claire). I have prayed this rosary many times and meditated on the suffering of Our Mother Mary. Our Lady saw her innocent and divine Son Jesus grow up and be crucified horribly, and she laid Him to rest. She was truly the Mother of us all. She continued to love us even though we sinned and did not follow her Son's will. Ilibagiza's other books were worth reading too to understand that deep and painful suffering is not isolated to only cancer patients.

An important book for me was *Divine Mercy Triumph Over Cancer: A Guide for Patients, Survivors and Their Caregivers*, by Ronald Sobecks. It discusses cancer through the lens of divine mercy. He was a faithful oncology doctor who documented how his patients embraced their diagnoses, upcoming death and faith. His book was a fantastic read, and when I read it again, I continued to see the things I myself discovered through my own cancer journey. Some books are worth reading several times. Reading a book once was sometimes not enough to fully capture and digest the lessons learned. Dr. Sobecks also discussed Our Lady's seven sorrows in his book.[29]

I also read *The Last Lecture* by Randy Pausch. He was a professor at Carnegie Mellon University who had liver cancer. He wrote about living life purposefully and about what he did with his family to make sure that they stayed strong together.

Anticancer: A Way of Life by Dr. David Servan-Schreiber gave a very honest and frank explanation about how one gets cancer and how it can be treated naturally. He was a cancer patient himself, and he passed away in 2011, after twenty years of battling with brain cancer. He said that

27 Ilibagiza. *Our Lady of Kibeho,* 151.

28 Ilibagiza. *Our Lady of Kibeho,* 186–198.

29 Ronald M. Sobecks, *Divine Mercy Triumph Over Cancer: A Guide for Patients, Survivors and Their Caregivers* (Stockbridge, Massachusetts: Marian Press, 2012), 151–152.

instead of positive thinking the realist's credo should be "what's most important is to always hope for the best but be prepared for the worst."[30]

In his book and DVD Dr. Servan-Schreiber discussed various foods for fighting cancer cells, like turmeric, chili peppers, green tea, etc. His book focused on three ways to manage cancer: 1) good nutrition, 2) regular physical exercise, and 3) managing stress.

In the book *What If You Could Skip the Cancer?* by Katrina Bos, who had breast cancer, I learned to follow the hierarchy of: 1) God, 2) self, 3) husband, 4) children, and 5) everyone and everything else (job, family, friends, neighbours, etc.).

In Regina Brett's book *God Never Blinks*, she discusses fifty lessons for life's little detours. For example, "Life is too short to waste time hating anyone" and "Life is too short for long pity parties. Get busy living, or get busy dying."[31]

Faith, Hope and Healing by Dr. Bernie Siegel tells inspiring stories about people living with cancer. Dr. Siegel added his own insights to the stories to help the readers appreciate the essence of the stories. His summations were insightful and inspiring. I enjoyed learning about others' journey with various forms of cancer. Siegel's book *101 Exercises for the Soul* was also very informative about how to have a healthy, body, mind, and spirit.

The books by Todd and Sonja Burpo tell of their three-year-old son dying and going to heaven. Their son, Colton, then returned to earth to slowly reveal what he had experienced in heaven. He saw Jesus. Each time his father asked Colton what Jesus looked like and showed him images, Colton would reply, "No, the hair's not right" or "The clothes aren't right."[32] One day, Colton's father received an email message with a painting done by an eight-year-old (Akiane Kramarik), whose mother was an

---

30 David Servan-Schrieber, *Anticancer: A New Way of Life* (London, UK: Collins, 2008).

31 Regina Brett, *God Never Blinks: 50 Lessons for Life's Little Detours* (New York: Grand Central Publishing, 2010).

32 Todd Burpo, *Heaven Is for Real: A Little Boy's Astounding Story of His Trip to Heaven and Back* (Nashville: HIFR Ministries, 2010), 93.

atheist. She was truly gifted and painted Jesus' portrait. When Colton saw Jesus' face on the computer screen he said, "Dad, that one's right."[33]

In his book Burpo included the image of Jesus, *Prince of Peace*, painted by Kramarik. I immediately loved the painting. I too felt that Jesus' eyes and hair looked realistic, and the realistic image really spoke to me. I loved the tenderness and mercy in Jesus' eyes.

I also enjoyed reading about near-death experiences. Joan Wester Anderson's book *An Angel to Watch Over Me: True Stories of Children's Encounter with Angels* describes many encounters of children with an angel. Jesus said in the Gospel of Matthew, "Let the children come to me, and do not prevent them; for the kingdom of heaven belongs to such as these" (Matthew 19:14).

The books by Lisa Elliot about her son's journey with leukemia are very inspirational. I could relate to the stages that she, as the mother of a cancer patient, went through. I was happy to meet her in London at her second book release. She is a strong and phenomenal person. Her son's courageous journey with cancer helped her and her family members to grow and strengthen their Christian faith.

The Painting Path—Embodying Spiritual Discovery through Yoga, Brush and Color by Linda Novick is an excellent summary of doing yoga poses, using a beginner's mind, and then following up with artful creations.

Motherhood Matters by Dorothy Pilarski was given to me by Ivan's aunt and cousin. The book made me reflect on my relationship with my mother and my daughter and inspired me to write to my mother for her seventy-fourth birthday and to list seventy-four things that I was grateful to her for.

Sister Patricia Proctor's book *101 Inspirational Stories of the Rosary* tells of many true situations where praying the rosary helped a person in a profound way. The rosary is a powerful prayer said to Our Mother Mary. Many people in desperate situations have prayed the rosary for their intentions to be heard by God through the intercession of His Mother Mary.

---

33 Burpo, *Heaven Is for Real,* 145.

Leaving Microsoft to Save the World by John Wood is an inspiring story of an executive who travelled to Nepal. He later left an excellent well-paying job to start-up Room To Read, a foundation to help increase literacy in financially poor nations, especially for women and young girls.

The following videos or seminars were helpful in my information gathering.

Cancer Care Talks are collaboratively hosted by Western University, London Regional Cancer Program (LRCP), Canadian Cancer Society Elgin-Middlesex, Wellspring Cancer Support Centre, and Canadian Institutes of Health Research. They are posted on the website at http://www.cancercaretalks.com/.

The DVD *Mummy Diaries* series from TV Ontario in 2008, recommended by the LRCP social worker, discusses how mothers facing cancer can prepare their children to cope with their death and afterwards. The video gives good ideas, tips, and stories. A counsellor helps the mothers to prepare a "treasure box" for their children. It's important for children to know that their mom loved them very much and it was not her choice to die; how to deal with issues like grief, friends, faith, change, and puberty; who they can go to who's trustworthy; how to keep their faith (very important); and how to make big decisions in life.

The DVD *The Ultimate Gift* is based on the book written by Jim Stovall, a blind person who "saw" that "life is a gift" of work, money, friends, learning, problems, family, laughter, dreams, giving, gratitude, a perfect day, and love. The quote that really hit home to me was "You don't begin to live until you've lost everything."

I watched a YouTube video about Leonardo da Vinci, the famous scientist and painter of the *Mona Lisa*. Da Vinci said, "While I thought I was learning how to live, I've been really learning how to die. As a day well spent brings happy sleep, so a life well used brings contented death." I really admired da Vinci (born 1452, died 1519) for all his wonderful paintings, drawings, anatomy sketches, and advanced thinking for his time.[34]

The following audio CD was also helpful. Jon Kabat-Zinn's *Mindfulness for Beginners* is rich with information about mindfulness and

---

34 *Leonardo da Vinci: Mona Lisa,* directed by Nick Rossiter (BBC UK Production, 2003, YouTube Video), 55:53 to 56:07.

meditation. He discusses awareness, being present in our lives, being non-judgmental, letting go, and having a beginner's mind.

All the noted books, videos, and CDs were key to shaping my attitude toward my cancer diagnosis and dealing with my own family and friends. These resources were worth exploring in detail because they expanded my perspective on my brain tumour and cancer and how to help my daughter grow and develop well.

42. COST OF CANCER TREATMENTS

*Life can be seen as an obstacle course filled with hurdles or
a marathon you are determined to complete.*

—Bernie Siegel[35]

WHEN I WAS DIAGNOSED WITH BRAIN CANCER, MY NEURO-ONCOLOGIST
suggested that I get approval in advance for my treatment drugs. We
initially encountered difficulties with the health insurance provider, but
fortunately we overcame the challenges so that my treatments could proceed without delay.

Here are the costs I've incurred to date (data has been taken from my
health care insurance benefits statements).

Reason	Cost
Ambulance for visit to North York General Hospital—December 2010	$ 45.00
Drugs administered at University Hospital—February 2011	$ 19.87
Private hospital room stay for ten days at University Hospital—February 2011	$ 2,280.00

35 Siegel, *101 Exercises for the Soul*, 177.

I also had prescriptions filled at the London Regional Cancer Program (LRCP) pharmacy that included (from the invoice report of March 1, 2011, to April 26, 2013) the following:

Type of Medication	Chemical Name (Brand Name)
Chemotherapy drugs	- Temozolomide - Lomustine
Antinauseants	- Ondansetron - Prochlorperazine (Stemetil) - Granisetron Hydrochloride
Anticonvulsants	- Phenytoin Sodium (Dilantin)

The medications filled at LRCP amounted to $39,510.47. This amount was for a period of approximately one year for Temodal, lomustine, and other drugs to treat side effects. I fortunately had an extremely good health care benefit plan; I paid a negligible amount of $36.

Each prescription had a $10 fee associated with it that amounted to $360 for the period cited.

Each day of chemotherapy with temozolomide and an antinauseant cost about $200. When I was taking lomustine and an antinauseant, the cost was about $75 each time.

I also had prescriptions filled at my local pharmacy, Shoppers Drug Mart (SDM). The medications filled at SDM were the following:

Type of Medication	Chemical Name (Brand Name)
Anticonvulsants	- Phenytoin Sodium (Dilantin) - Levetiracetem (Keppra)

From the period of February 18, 2011, to July 26, 2015, the total costs were $22,846.63. This included a dispensing fee of typically $11.99 per transaction and my contribution to date of a negligible, again, $21.00.

A typical refill consists of 360 tablets for 250 mg of Keppra, which costs $723.18 or $2 per tablet. A typical refill would last me ninety days, or three months. I take four tablets of Keppra each day.

Other Costs

There were also other financial costs to consider. For example, other over-the-counter (non-prescription) drugs, like the following:

- Advil
- Extra Strength Tylenol
- Gravol
- Lactulose

There were also medical team costs, like the following:

- surgical costs for my craniotomy and Caesarean section
- the time of the medical team of oncologists, nurses, surgeons, phlebotomists, etc.
- needles, bandages, hospital costs, and facility services
- "behind the scenes" costs like the radiation dosimetrists, medical physicists, neuro-radiologists, engineering technicians, computer programmers, etc., involved in preparing and analyzing all my radiation, MRI and CT scans
- The time to arrange MRI appointment bookings for me and my follow-up with my medical team

There were travel costs, like the following:

- hospital parking fees for every radiation session, MRI appointment and follow-up appointment with the oncologists

- time off work for my husband to accompany me to all my appointments
- fuel costs for all the travel back and forth from home to the hospital and also to the pharmacy for prescriptions

In summary, the financial cost of cancer is not insignificant. So far, the costs of my hospital stay and treatments alone amount to at least $64,700. I have had twenty MRI scans since 2011 and at least as many appointments with my oncologists. The MRIs and oncologist visits will continue to increase.

The cost of pain and suffering of those who have helped me cannot be calculated from a financial point of view. Suffice it to say, cancer affects everyone with whom the patient interacts. Cancer is not isolated to an individual. Although it is an individual who is directly impacted by cancer, the families and friends also bear a similar pain and loss that cannot be calculated.

PART 3
HOW I GOT IT

When I learned that I had terminal cancer, I was in shock and awe. I didn't realize at the time that cancer was truly a gift of learning for me. Through my cancer and motherhood journey, I learned a lot about myself and changed some of my views and attitudes about life.

43. Lessons Learned from My Journey

Here I summarize my lessons learned and new discoveries.

Physical

Doing meditation, yoga, t'ai chi and qi gong at Wellspring helped me balance my physical well-being. Keeping my mind and physical body strong, focused, and centred helped my healing. Learning to breathe well in yoga helped me to calm down, relax, and take one day at a time. I firmly believe that stress is part of cancer. I learned to de-stress by taking deep long breaths and reduced my multitasking. I didn't try so hard anymore to please everyone. It was burning me out and sucking away my energy. I needed to refocus on my well-being and reprioritized my efforts and energy for situations that really mattered in the "bigger picture" of life.

Eating healthy anti-cancer foods helped tremendously to heal my body. I consciously had more water, fruits, and vegetables. I also tried to walk to church during the week and to do physical exercise. I also rested a lot. I knew rest (not just a nap) was very important for my cells to rejuvenate and grow back.

Spiritual

I developed a stronger faith and belief in prayer. Many people prayed for my family. I realized that God is always in control and God gave us free will to make our own decisions. I truly believe that God hears our prayers. We have to be humble and patient enough to see, hear, and recognize His presence in our busy lives. I truly believe that through the prayers of so many people in my life, God really heard and understood our petition for a "miracle." I often say that a miracle already happened. Even though I had terminal cancer, I gave birth to a healthy baby. Each day I am alive is a miracle in itself. I can't complain to anyone, especially not to God. To complain is to appear ungrateful. I am certainly very grateful to have life and see my daughter growing.

Mental

I realized that my mental health has to include balancing expectations, breathing well, de-stressing, reducing high expectations for myself, and shedding the perfectionism attitude ingrained in me. I recognized that I have to let go when enough is enough. I changed and learned to feel satisfied with less than 100 percent. I learned to balance effort with desired outcomes and that sometimes spending more time and effort reduces the productivity. Simplifying is best. I really needed to declutter and simplify all the activities I dealt with. I learned that I really couldn't control other people's attitudes, and I learned to stay away from people who bring negative energy to me (who complain about matters that I and they can't control). I found that negative people are "energy suckers" and only bring others down.

I also prepared myself mentally by reading several relevant books to dispel the myths that I heard from many "unofficial" sources. Reading helped me to stay calm and be prepared for my treatments.

While recovering from treatments, I did not work. I was able to de-stress by not needing to check and respond to messages from work on my BlackBerry. I took the time to rest and not feel guilty about relaxing at nights and on the weekends. I consciously decided that I did not need to be accessible all the time to everybody.

Social

I got to know my true family and friends. Sadly, I realized that some of them were only really there for their own selfish reasons rather than to help me. I fully realize and appreciate now that we affect everyone we meet in life, and there are no coincidences. I learned to appreciate what I have and also what I do not have.

I also learned to be humble when asking for help. It was not easy to ask for help. Even though I liked to be independent, I knew I couldn't manage everything, like going to appointments and taking care of Genevieve. As time went on, I learned to accept help from others. I found that others really want to feel useful.

As part of de-stressing, I had to re-evaluate my priorities with social gatherings, and Ivan and I decided that we didn't need to go to every family event that was two hours away. We also didn't need to stress about getting and buying the most appropriate gift. It was important to simplify all my activities. After I stopped worrying so much about physical and temporal things, I realized that prayers are the best gift for another loved one who is truly in need.

I learned that it is important to make sure my connections with my family and friends are sound. I realized that connections are vitally important in life. When the situations were difficult, reliable and loving family and friends helped us tremendously with prayers, food, and care for Genevieve.

Cancer does not affect just the patient. The caregivers, families, and friends too are very much affected by a cancer diagnosis. It's just as important that the caregivers and friends do not burn out from trying to fix or deal with someone or something that is impossible to treat.

Psychological

I came to realize (very painfully) truths that were hard to accept about my family and friends. I recognized that all my past actions still had present consequences. I always worked very hard, and even after ten years, my boss still remembered me and sponsored me for our first Spring Sprint to raise money for the Brain Tumour Foundation of Canada.

I was fortunate that I didn't have to make choices about my surgery, chemotherapy, and radiation. When I lost consciousness, immediate surgery was the only option. After surgery, there was no choice but to immediately commence chemotherapy and radiation together. We didn't have to agonize about the various options and outcomes. The severity of my brain tumour necessitated immediate actions.

Personal Self-Awareness

I had to accept my life and all the decisions I made and their consequences. Life boils down to personal responsibility. We have to look at our choices and decisions before pointing at others. Being my own health advocate, with Ivan's help, and confident in my choices, with the help and grace of Jesus and Mother Mary I've survived having cancer and being a new mother at the same time.

44. HAVING A DIFFERENT APPROACH TO LIFE

EACH DAY, I TOOK AN APPROACH WHERE I LOOKED AT ONE DAY AT A TIME. SOME days and some planning seemed so overwhelming that I had to step back and say, "Do only what you can handle; be honest and realistic."

Having a Sense of Humour

Genevieve often came up with the funniest things to say to us, and I wrote them in a little book so that she can laugh when she's older. For example, she said at two years old, "When I was young…" She was so young, and yet she knew she was getting older as each day passed.

I always enjoyed art therapy sessions. As we were creating our pieces, we chatted and laughed about many things, especially about ourselves. I always felt better after a good hearty laugh. We oxygenate our whole bodies when we laugh, and laughing is always very refreshing to the body and mind.

Sharing My Story and Being Appreciative

While it was difficult to go through my notes and recall all that my family had been through since early 2011, when organizing my thoughts on paper I felt healing taking place.

Ivan and I were one of the first to share our story on the Brain Tumour Foundation of Canada website to promote fundraising for the Spring Sprint 2012. Since then, the website has been filled with personal stories from survivors and caregivers. Ivan and I were happy that we had inspired others to share their personal stories.

I also shared my story with my parish in our newspaper in Easter 2013. Some families who were also in Genevieve's daycare approached me after the article was published because they didn't know that I had terminal cancer. They also offered their help to us.

Our pastor invited me to share my story with the Precious Blood Sisters. He also asked me to speak at a retreat on August 21, 2013, at the Our Lady of the Rosary Shrine in Merlin, Ontario. On the bus ride back to London, many people approached me to say how they were inspired by my story.

Each week at Wellspring, someone would ask, "How are you doing, and how's Genevieve?" I always spoke proudly about Genevieve and the funny things she was doing. As for my condition, I remain positive and try not to complain and just appreciate that I am alive.

Believing in Prayers

I truly believe that my relatively good health was all due to the many prayers from family, friends, and strangers. The masses, prayers, and intentions that were raised to Divine Mercy Jesus and Our Lady of Guadalupe helped me, Ivan, and Genevieve to survive.

In 2011, when we received my pathology results, I was so upset that I might not see Genevieve go to junior kindergarten, but in September 2015 she started attending a French Catholic school. I am so grateful to everyone on our journey for their prayers and good wishes. I am totally indebted to all my family and friends who have supported Ivan, Genevieve, and me on our brain cancer and new parenting journey.

Above all, I am abundantly grateful to Divine Mercy Jesus and Our Lady of Guadalupe for answering our prayers for a miracle. The birth of a healthy Genevieve was truly a miracle in itself. Every day I am alive is truly a miracle, and I am eternally grateful to God, my Saviour Jesus Christ, who loves us unconditionally, and His merciful and loving Mother Mary.

Jesus said in the Gospel of St. Matthew, "Ask and it will be given to you; seek and you will find; knock and the door will be opened to you. For everyone who asks, receives; and the one who seeks, finds; and to the one who knocks, the door will be opened" (Matthew 7:7–8).

Pope Francis said, "God loves us with a free and boundless love" when he referred to the Gospel of St. John 3:16 where it is written, "For

God so loved the world that he gave his only Son, so that everyone who believes in him might not perish but might have eternal life."

Although I started my cancer journey and my motherhood journey by not "getting it," in time, I learned to "get it." Both my journeys continue, and I feel stronger to face the challenges ahead. I had the time to reflect and look back on what's worked. I slowed down, stopped, paused, and reflected about what my journey taught me. Having cancer enriched my life in a positive way. At first I thought the worst when I heard "cancer." As I look back, I see that if cancer had not affected my life so drastically, I would have missed significant lessons about life. As Mother Teresa said, "Silence will teach us a lot. It will teach us to speak with Christ and to speak joyfully to our brothers and sisters."[36]

My final advice: embrace life and all its ups and downs. Life is always full of surprises and new lessons. God is always in control of our lives. We need to trust God and His Mother to help us through our high times and low times. My question to you is, do you get it?

---

36 Quoted in González-Balado, *Mother Teresa*, 11.

References

Anderson, Joan Wester. *An Angel to Watch Over Me: True Stories of Children's Encounters with Angels*. Chicago, Illinois: Loyola Press, 2012.

Béliveau, Richard, and Denis Gingras. *Foods That Fight Cancer: Preventing Cancer through Diet*. Translated by Miléna Stojonac. Toronto, Ontario: McClelland & Stewart, 2005. Originally published as *Les aliments contre le cancer* (Outremont, Quebec: Éditions du Trécarré, 2005).

Bos, Katrina. *What If You Could Skip the Cancer?* Northville, MI: Ferne Press, 2009.

Bowden, Jonny. *The 150 Healthiest Foods on Earth: The Surprising, Unbiased Truth About What You Should Eat and Why*. Beverly, Massachusetts: Fair Winds Press, 2007.

Brett, Regina. *God Never Blinks: 50 Lessons for Life's Little Detours*. New York: Grand Central Publishing, 2010.

Burpo, Todd, and Sonja Burpo. *Heaven Changes Everything: Living Every Day with Eternity in Mind*. Nashville: Thomas Nelson, 2012.

Burpo, Todd, with Lynn Vincent. *Heaven Is for Real: A Little Boy's Astounding Story of His Trip to Heaven and Back*. Nashville: HIFR Ministries, 2010.

De Souza, Lin-Pei. "A Faith Filled Journey: Having A Newborn Child and Brain Cancer." *Family Matters* 7, no. 1 (Easter 2013), newspaper of Holy Family Parish, London, Ontario.

Elliott, Lisa. *Dancing in the Rain: One Family's Journey through Grief and Loss*. Winnipeg: Word Alive Press, 2014.

Elliott, Lisa. *The Ben Ripple: Choosing to Live Through Loss with Purpose*. Winnipeg: Word Alive Press, 2012.

Gast, David. *Musing and Muttering…Through Cancer*. Winnipeg: Word Alive Press, 2008.

González-Balado, José Luis, comp. *Mother Teresa: In My Own Words*. Toronto: Random House, 1996.

Ilibagiza, Immaculée, with Steve Irwin. *Our Lady of Kibeho: Mary Speaks to the World from the Heart of Africa*. Carlsbad, CA: Hay House, 2008.

Ilibagiza, Immaculée, with Steve Erwin. *The Boy Who Met Jesus: Segatashya of Kibeho*. Carlsbad, CA: Hay House, 2011.

Ilibagiza, Immaculée, with Steve Erwin. *The Rosary: The Prayer That Saved My Life*. Carlsbad, CA: Hay House, 2013.

Michalenko, Seraphim, et al. *The Divine Mercy: Message and Devotion: With Selected Prayers from the Diary of St. Maria Faustina Kowalska*, rev. ed. Stockbridge, Massachusetts: Marian Press, 2001.

Nouwen, Henri. *Can You Drink The Cup?* New York: Ave Maria Press, 1996.

Nouwen, Henri. *Finding My Way Home: Pathways to Life and the Spirit*. New York: The Crossroad Publishing Company, 2001.

Nouwen, Henri. *Our Greatest Gift: A Meditation on Dying and Caring*. New York: Harper Collins, 1994.

Novick, Linda. *The Painting Path: Embodying Spiritual Discovery through Yoga, Brush and Color*. Woodstock, VT: SkyLight Paths Publishing, 2007.

Pausch, Randy. *The Last Lecture*. New York: Hyperion Press, 2008.

Pilarski, Dorothy. *Motherhood Matters: Inspirational Stories, Letters, Quotes & Prayers for Catholic Moms*. Toronto: Catholic Register Books, 2011.

Proctor, Patricia. *101 Inspirational Stories of the Rosary*. Spokane, Washington: Franciscan Monastery of Saint Clare, 2003.

Roloff, Tricia Ann, ed. *Navigating Through a Strange Land: A Book for Brain Tumor Patients and Their Families*. West Fork, AR: Indigo Press, 1994.

Rutledge, Rob, and Timothy Walker. *The Healing Circle: Integrating Science, Wisdom and Compassion in Reclaiming Wholeness on the Cancer Journey*. Halifax, Nova Scotia: The Healing and Cancer Foundation, 2010.

Scientific American. *What You Need to Know About Cancer: Scientific American, A Special Issue*. USA: W. H. Freeman and Company, 1997.

Servan-Schrieber, David. *Anticancer: A New Way of Life*. London, UK: Collins, 2008.

Siegel, Bernie S. *101 Exercises for the Soul: Simple Practices for a Healthy, Body, Mind & Spirit*. Novato, California: New World Library, 2005.

Siegel, Bernie, and Jennifer Sander. *Faith, Hope & Healing: Inspiring Lessons Learned from People Living With Cancer*. Hoboken, New Jersey: Wiley, 2009.

Sobecks, Ronald M. *Divine Mercy Triumph Over Cancer: A Guide for Patients, Survivors and Their Caregivers*. Stockbridge, MA: Marian Press, 2012.

Taylor, Jill Bolte. *My Stroke of Insight: A Brain Scientist's Personal Journey*. New York: Penguin Random House, 2008.

The Academy of the Immaculate. *A Handbook On Guadalupe*. Waite Park, MN: Parke Press, 2001.

The Reader's Digest. *Food Cures: Breakthrough Nutritional Prescriptions for Everything From Colds to Cancer, 1st Canadian Edition*. Montreal, QC: The Reader's Digest Association (Canada) ULC, 2007.

The Reader's Digest. *Foods That Harm, Food That Heal: The Best and Worst Choices to Treat Your Ailments Naturally*. White Plains, NY: The Reader's Digest Association, 2013.

Wood, John. *Leaving Microsoft to Change the World*. New York: Collins, 2006.

Appendix

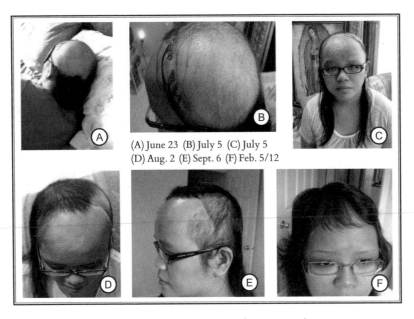

(A) June 23 (B) July 5 (C) July 5
(D) Aug. 2 (E) Sept. 6 (F) Feb. 5/12

Fig. 1 – Hair Loss Progression (2011 to 2012)

Fig. 2 – Lili-Fei and Ivan at the Basilica of Our Lady of Guadalupe (Mexico, 2010)

Fig. 3 – Close up image of Our Lady's abdomen

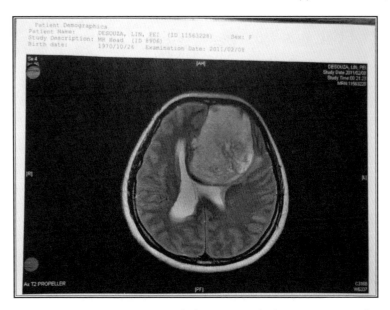

Fig. 4 – Brain MRI scan pre-surgery (February 8, 2011) – large mass on top right is the tumour; in an MRI scan, the left side of the brain appears as the right side

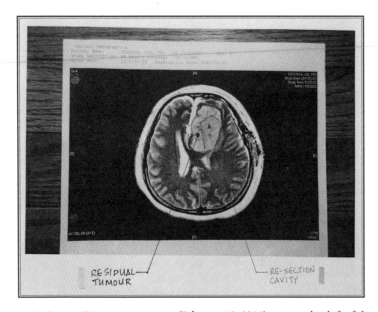

Fig. 5 – Brain MRI scan post-surgery (February 10, 2011) – notice the shift of the centreline after surgery. The entry point for surgery was from the left side of my head (shown on the right side of the scan). The pink section highlights where the tumour was removed. The green section highlights the remaining (or residual) tumour after surgery.

Fig. 6 – My "Soul Scape" developed during the Soul Medicine program at LRCP

Seven Chakras
Aug. 29, 2013
Marker, coloured pencils

Fig. 7 – Mandala creation from Art Therapy

My Special Place
June 19, 2014
Placemat, acrylic paint

Fig. 8 – Painting on a circular placemat to represent my key desires: love, faith, family and friends

The Continuation
July 24, 2014
Black marker

Fig. 9 – Using a small image (upper right hand side), I created and extended it to design and create a new image

A Cosmic Place
2014
Acrylic paint on newspaper

Fig. 10 – Feeling free to paint on newspaper, I created a cosmic place full of bright colours

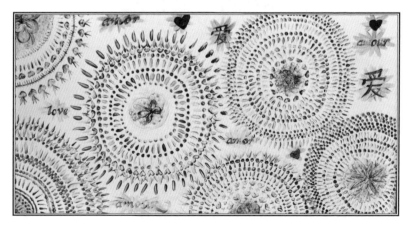

Fig. 11 – Image of my "Loving Eternity" panel at St. Joseph's Hospital, London (2013)

Fig. 12 – Final portable labyrinth ready for inaugural walk at Wellspring yoga studio